LIVING
IN JESUS

WOMEN OF FAITH™
STUDY GUIDE SERIES

LIVING
IN JESUS

FOREWORD BY
MARILYN
MEBERG

THOMAS NELSON PUBLISHERS
Nashville

✦ CONTENTS ✦

LIVING
IN JESUS

✦ FOREWORD ✦

My mother paid me to eat. I was so skinny it was a bad witness for my pastor-father's ministry. It wasn't that the food at my house was bad, I just wasn't interested in food. Eating interfered with my outdoor activities and my indoor other-mindedness. As I look back on my mother's desperation to feed me at least a quarter's worth of something, I feel empathy for her concern and admiration for her creativity.

Of course I'd have a hefty bankroll if I were paid for my food consumption now. One of my most favorite activities in life is fine dining. When Ken and I could finally afford it, our dinners out became a contest. One time Ken would choose the restaurant as well as the menu for both of us. (He knew my tastes and never ordered liver or fish.) The next meal out I'd choose the restaurant as well as his menu selection. After three times we'd vote on who chose the best restaurant and menu. The winner got a prize . . . a free meal! (I guess eating and money are still connected for me.)

What are your fine dining inclinations? Whatever your style or preference I know for a certainty, it's time for you to put on some weight. You are undoubtedly thin—too thin. How do I know that? Because I also become too thin from time to time and need fattening up. We do not want to stay in that state of "bad-witness" scrawniness. There's a sumptuous solution to our scrawniness! It does not require we save our quarters; it's inexpensive as well as fun!

What in the world am I talking about? It's this. You are holding in your hands an incredible Bible study. Its intention is to fatten you up on spiritual nutrients. Not only will you deepen your understanding of what "Living in Christ" means, you won't change dress sizes.

This study will help you comprehend what happens after you receive Jesus into your life. The Bible says "Those who become Christians become new persons. They are not the same anymore, for the old life is gone. A new life has begun!" (2 Cor. 5:17) Now that dear ones, is a fat-producing truth. But what does it mean? We may be relieved at the promise our old life is gone since it wasn't working well much of the time anyway, but if it's gone . . . what became of it? Perhaps in the quietness of your heart you're pretty sure it's still hanging around. In fact, most of the time it doesn't appear to be gone at all.

Let me give you a fattening appetizer verse for you to munch on:

"For you have been born again. Your new life did not come from your earthly parents because the life they gave you will end in death. But this new life will last forever because it comes from the eternal, living word of God." (1 Peter 1:23)

I called this verse an appetizer because this study will begin the meal that fattens your soul and feeds your understandings about your new life in Christ.

You may want to begin this study with other equally skinny persons where your individual weight gain can be observed and congratulated by each other. If on the other hand, time or inclination causes you to do this study on your own, go for it! You'll get fat no matter how few or how many persons are at the table with you.

Just know for a certainty your life will never be the same once you've entered into your new life with Christ. No matter how things appear to you on the outside you are a new creature on the inside. In feeding that new life, all of us need to maintain a high caloric intake of the nutrients God wants to feed us from His Word.

— *Marilyn Meberg*

✦ INTRODUCTION ✦

*Those who become Christians become new persons. They are not the same anymore,
for the old life is gone. A new life has begun!*

2 Corinthians 5:17, NLT

Have you ever read books just to escape the never-ending dullness of
everyday life? Through the chapters of some paperback, we experience
the shadows of an existence that seems more interesting, more exciting,
more appealing than what our own day has to offer. Damsels find unfailing love, sleuths seek out elusive clues, strangers form unlikely alliances,
adventurers cross unfamiliar terrains, and they all live happily ever after.
In comparison, we feel boring, listless, and wistful.

Little do we realize that as believers, we have been ushered into a life
that rivals the plot of any mere story! We have become leading ladies in
a thrilling tale of epic proportions. There's something for everyone: combat, romance, intrigue, drama, rescue, duplicity, character development,
action, adventure, complex subplots, moral dilemmas, sacrifice, tear jerk-
ing, subtle humor, slapstick, subterfuge, betrayal, showdowns, discovery,
unexpected twists, irony, paradise, and a happy ending.

The Christian life is vibrant, mysterious, and beautiful. In a
word—sensational! Open your eyes to the wonder of a life knit with the
divine. Jesus has called you, chosen you, changed you. Your life is caught
up with His, transformed into something altogether new. Jesus is your
intimate friend—familiar, inseparable, precious. He has called you His
beloved, and made you fantastic promises. Your life is a never-ending
story that will continue to unfold throughout eternity.

All because of what you are in *Him.*

*"In Christ we have a love that can never be fathomed, a life that can never die, a joy
that can never be diminished, a hope that can never be disappointed, a purity that
can never be defiled, and resources that can never be exhausted."*

Barbara Johnson

"We live in Him. We walk in Him. We are in Him."

Acts 17:28, NCV

CHAPTER 1

ALIVE IN HIM

"IN CHRIST ALL SHALL BE MADE ALIVE."

1 Corinthians 15:22, NKJV

Did you wake up today feeling alive? Do you face each dawn with the enthusiastic motto, "You only live once, so make it count!" Do you frequently sigh, "Ahhhhh. This is the life." A life worth living! Or is it?

We talk about living—living dangerously, living large, living high, living it up. We claim a right to life. We work to make a living. Some of us live in the past, while others live for tomorrow. We live and learn. We live and let live. We have livable expectations. Our homes have lived-in looks. What more could we ask?

It's easy to get wrapped up in our day-to-day living. The world we live in is quite authentic—it is all we have ever known. But we forget this life is fleeting in comparison to the eternity that lies ahead. Paul says that our *real* life is hidden with God in Christ (Col. 3:3, NLT).

CLEARING ✦ THE ✦ COBWEBS

Does your house have a living room? Why do you suppose it's called that? What is *your* living room used for?

1. Life is a gift from God. He created us, and He made each of us unique. Job declared, "The breath of the Almighty gives me life" (Job 33:4, NKJV). What does Isaiah 42:5 say? *This is what God the Lord says — he who created the heavens and stretched them out, who spread out the earth and all that comes out of it, who gives breath to its people, and life to those who walk on it.*

2. And so we are born. Beautiful babies are brought into this world every day. But the taint of sin touches each new life. How is this described in Ephesians 2:1? *And you he made alive, who were dead in trespasses & sins*

> When a person comes to God, just as she is—while still in her sinning state—God looks at her and, because of what Jesus Christ did on the Cross, He proclaims her righteous. She does not have to clean up her act. She does not have to do penance. She does not have to be thin or good-looking or rich or famous or accomplished. All she has to do is believe God for the forgiveness of her sins.
>
> Luci Swindoll

3. God didn't stop with giving us life on earth. A handful of decades was not enough. He prepared an extraordinary gift for the faithful. What is it? Read 1 John 5:11. *eternal life — this life is in this son*

4. So there is this life on earth, which we are born to. Then there is our new life, which remains hidden in Christ for now. How does Peter compare these two kinds of living in 1 Peter 1:23? *because we were born again not of perishable seed, but imperishable*

5. Romans 6:11 says that we are now "dead to sin" and "alive to God." Quite a transformation! What other changes have taken place? Consider Paul's words in 2 Corinthians 5:15–17.

he died so we live for him not ourselves

if we live in Christ - the old is gone & we are a new creation

6. What hope! Look at the promise reworded in the letter to the Romans—Romans 8:10.

But if Christ is in you, your body is dead because of sin, yet your spirit is alive because of righteousness

7. What direction does Paul give to Christians in living out this new life?

Remember Elijah? There was a time when he was heartsick and footsore and feeling very alone. He wanted desperately to hear a word from God. He needed His touch. So he sat up and watched for Him. Elijah thought God would come in a whirlwind, but He didn't. Elijah looked for God in an earthquake, but He wasn't there either. Next, he listened for God in the midst of a great fire, but God did not speak from it. In the end, Elijah found a little whisper tickling his ears—rather anticlimactic after the empty showmanship he had witnessed. But that quiet voice was just what Elijah had needed (1 Kin. 19:11–12).

God works many miracles in this world, and He reaches out to touch the weary and the hurting. But God doesn't always come in with a bang these days. He doesn't need to! Do you know the song that says, "You're the only Jesus some may ever see"? Or how about that wonderful chorus that goes "We are His hands, we are His feet." Though our efforts to lift one another up may seem anticlimactic after the Lord's ministry on this earth, it is just what your hurting sisters need. In quiet ways we can show God's love, and that love can work real miracles!

8. What else does Paul say about "the life I now live"? Look in Galatians 2:20.

I no longer live, but Christ lives in me

> I need intimate contact with God. Our souls were made for this. When we deprive our souls of that very life force, we can survive—but that is all we are doing. We were not created to merely survive but to thrive in God.
>
> Sheila Walsh

9. What does this mean? How does Christ live *through* you?

actions things I do for others

10. We are alive in Christ, and eternal life will be the reward we receive from our loving Heavenly Father. How does Romans 2:7 describe the faithful believers who receive this gift of life?

in doing good seek glory & honor

✦ DIGGING DEEPER ✦

There seems to be a running theme through the Book of John about eternal life. Many verses there speak about our never-ending future with God. Let's explore a few of them here.

- John 1:4
- John 3:36
- John 6:40
- John 6:47
- John 10:28
- John 11:25
- John 14:6
- John 17:3

✦ PONDER & PRAY ✦

Thank the Lord this week, for you are alive! The life you now live will stretch out into eternity, and you will dwell in the presence of the Lord forever! Amen! As you walk through the week ahead of you, ask God to show you small ways in which you can change the lives of those around you. By reaching out to your sisters in Christ, Christ lives through you. Then, consider how Jesus would reach out to others in your circle of influence—husband, children, parents, neighbors, coworkers, friends, acquaintances, and strangers. Is God calling you to share life with them?

✦ TRINKETS TO TREASURE ✦

At the close of every Women of Faith conference, women are asked to play a little game of pretend. Each conference guest is asked to imagine that a gift has been placed in their hands—one from each of the speakers. These gifts serve as reminders of the different lessons shared by the Women of Faith. This study guide will carry on this tradition! At the close of each lesson, you will be presented with a small gift. Though imaginary, it will serve to remind you of the things you have learned. Think of it as a souvenir. Souvenirs are little trinkets we pick up on our journeys to remind us of where we have been. They keep us from forgetting the path we have traveled. Hide these little treasures in your heart, for as you ponder on them, they will draw you closer to God.

✦ TRINKETS TO TREASURE ✦

Our trinket to treasure this week simply must be something alive. So you must have an ivy cutting—a living gift to remind you that you are alive in Christ. If you care for it properly, your ivy will grow and flourish, filling out and sending fresh tendrils of greenery around it. Then, you will be able to take cuttings from your own full-grown plant and give them to more friends. They can then pass along cuttings to their friends. You see, sharing ivy cuttings is a lot like sharing our faith—spreading love and life to those around us. In this way, Christ lives through us!

✦ NOTES & PRAYER REQUESTS ✦

CHAPTER 2

HIDDEN IN HIM

"YOUR LIFE IS HIDDEN WITH CHRIST IN GOD"

Colossians 3:3, NKJV

My children hide from me sometimes. They are looking for a safe haven when they think I will be upset with them. The crash of breaking glass is usually followed by the sounds of scurrying feet, then sudden silence. The culprits must be coaxed out from behind chairs and under beds before their explanations can be heard. It's not always fleeing the scene of the crime, though. My kids love to grab their blankets and flashlights and shut themselves into their closets, pretending to be campers or whispering plans for a secret birthday gift. Sometimes they hide from me just for the sheer joy of surprising me—I guess they like the fleeting glimpse of astonishment when they jump at me from around corners. My absolute favorite hider, though, is the one-year-old amateur. These are the children who believe, for some strange reason, if they cannot see you, you cannot see them. My son once tried to crawl across my bedroom floor on knees and elbows, hands firmly pressed against his eyes. He was completely convinced of his invisibility as he passed by in plain sight.

CLEARING
✦ THE ✦
COBWEBS

Did you have a special place where you kept your childhood treasures? How did you keep it hidden from everyone?

There are times when I want to hide, too. Sometimes I long for a few hours of blessed quietness. Many of us have burdens we'd like to sneak away from for a time — pain, worry, fears, stress, memories, heartbreak, expectations, homesickness, loneliness, addictions, overwhelming responsibilities, sorrow. When we feel the urge to run away, we don't really have far to go. God welcomes us with open arms, and He can be our hiding place.

> *I have learned that sometimes we will be aware of His closeness and sometimes we won't. At times we experience the sweetness of God's nearness and at other times the frightening loneliness of His distance. The Lord hasn't changed locations, but we might have become caught up in our own agendas and forgotten His presence and availability. Other times the Lord will be silently still (scary) for holy purposes (awesome) we don't understand (frustrating), yet . . . (hallelujah).*
>
> Patsy Clairmont

1. Have you ever had a time when you desperately wanted a place to hide?

2. When David wanted to hide, where did he turn? Read Psalm 59:16 and 91:2.

3. God is a safe place for believers. He is always near. What does Jesus promise in Matthew 28:20?

4. Nothing is hidden from God, yet He is able to tuck us away, safeguarding us from the enemy. What does Hebrews 4:13 say about the watchful eye of our Lord?

5. In the days just before He was crucified, Jesus offered up a prayer for His disciples. What did He ask of His Father in John 17:11–16?

> *Our God is the all-knowing One who sees our scars, our secrets, and our strength. Our wounds and shame are His affair, and He knows just how much trouble we can stand. Somehow, the fact that He knows us so well makes a difference. We understand there is a direction and we are part of a bigger picture. From the wilderness in our lives, the fact that He sees gives us a reason to carry on. No longer are we anonymous, lonely, and lost.*
>
> Barbara Johnson

6. What else is hidden in Christ? Look up Colossians 2:3.

There are two different ways to go about decorating a home, as far as I'm concerned. One way is to decorate for others. The other is to decorate for yourself. You know you're only decorating for others when all the pretty things in your house are out where people can see them. I prefer to suit myself, even if nobody else will ever see my creations. I have painted the insides of drawers in daring shades of green. I have color-coordinated my laundry room. My prettiest birdfeeder is tucked away in the back yard, where even my neighbors cannot see it. It doesn't bother me that nobody sees my hidden treasures. I see them! Their beauty gives me joy.

How much more care should we take in putting the finishing touches on our hidden person—our soul? If you spend all your time decorating the outside of yourself, then you are just decorating

> *Do you ever feel as if you are killing yourself serving your children and your husband or your church or your friends, but no one seems to notice or appreciate you? I believe we women need to resist that type of thinking. It's so discouraging—and it's so untrue! God sees our hearts, and that's all He cares about. He doesn't miss a single moment of a life lived out for Him.*
>
> Sheila Walsh

for others. You are putting on a show, but all the while you are hiding dusty drawers and empty closets. Though nobody but God will ever see the hidden places of your heart, don't neglect that part. Beautify your hidden spots, and the results will be precious in the eyes of God.

7. God is concerned about your hidden parts. He knows you intimately. What does He desire to find in your secret places? Consider 1 Peter 3:4 before answering.

8. Our heart is a holy place, for it is where we meet God! What else can be hidden in your heart? Psalm 119:11 makes an invaluable suggestion.

> Holy moments come to us daily if we will ask for eyes to see. It may be the sun streaming through the window as you fold laundry. Or maybe it's lifting your friends to God while you vacuum. We can't always withdraw to quiet hillsides to pray, but Christ will meet with us in the quiet places of our hearts.
>
> Sheila Walsh

9. Psalm 51:6 holds a promise concerning our hidden parts. What does David assert?

10. Only those things which are hidden in Christ will last forever. Read Jesus' Words in Matthew 6:20 and Luke 12:33. What things in your life are safe in Christ's hands? What will happen to the rest?

✦ DIGGING DEEPER ✦

The Psalms are filled with references to God as a hiding place, a shelter, a safe haven. These verses hold promises, each a precious reminder that you are in God's protection and care.

- Psalm 3:5
- Psalm 16:9
- Psalm 17:8
- Psalm 18:19
- Psalm 27:5
- Psalm 57:1
- Psalm 61:2
- Psalm 94:22
- Psalm 144:2

✦ PONDER & PRAY ✦

If you find yourself longing for a hiding place this week, run to God. Reread all of His promises to be your shelter, and pray for the peace of His refuge. Please spend time this week giving your own hidden places some consideration. Take to heart the Psalmist's words in Psalm 119:11, and begin to hide God's Word in your heart. This would be a wonderful time to begin a systematic Scripture memorization plan. It doesn't take much effort, but you will carry those Words with you into eternity. They will be treasures indeed.

✦ TRINKETS TO TREASURE ✦

We are hidden in Christ, and the security of that safe place fills our hearts with confidence and joy. So this week's little gift is something for you to hide. Have you been introduced to Barbara Johnson's little "splashes of joy"—iridescent bits of glass that look like splashed water on your windowsill? I want you to take a few of these and tuck them into places where only you will see them. These hidden baubles will decorate your hidden places, just as God's Word and a gentle spirit beautify your hidden places. When you come across a joy splash during your day, thank God for His care—and smile!

✦ NOTES & PRAYER REQUESTS ✦

CHAPTER 3

ROOTED IN HIM

"WICKEDNESS NEVER BRINGS STABILITY; ONLY THE GODLY HAVE DEEP ROOTS"

Proverbs 12:3, NLT

Tree lots are a familiar sight during the holiday season. They crop up in every vacant lot, surrounded by makeshift fences with bare bulbs strung around their perimeter. They are like little forests in the middle of busy neighborhoods. Scotch pines, Douglas firs, blue spruce—evergreens of every description are lined up. The scents are amazing. Fresh, green, balsam scents. It's the smell of Christmas.

The tree lot trees are vibrant, fragrant, and appealing. They give life to the otherwise dismal days of winter. Some of the trees have even been sprayed in the fields, giving them a startlingly green hue—sort of like Astroturf. But for all their glossy needles and forest fragrances, the tree lot trees are doomed to fade. Every woman knows this, for she must man the vacuum cleaner. Every day that passes brings a fresh shower of needles on the carpet, and once the holidays are past, a tree lot tree is only good for the wood chipper.

Tree lot trees are pretty things, and they brighten our festivities during the holidays. But they cannot

CLEARING ✦ THE ✦ COBWEBS

Would you say that you have a green thumb? Do you have a favorite houseplant? A favorite flower? A favorite tree?

last, for they have been cut. Even an *ever*green cannot go on without the nourishment it received from its roots.

1. Several times in the Scriptures, the righteous man is compared to a thriving tree. Consider Psalm 1:3 and Jeremiah 17:8. What is the source of these trees' abundance?

> Jesus said, "Follow Me." He never instructed us to follow each other's rules. He never gave anyone control over another. His desire is that His Word and His Spirit be our guides for life. Being a follower of Jesus Christ means becoming more and more like Him—letting His Spirit transform us into all we were created to be. That happens, dear friend, from the inside out.
>
> Luci Swindoll

2. Similarly, we are to be rooted in Christ. Where does Colossians 2:7 say our roots should lead?

3. From where do our roots draw their strength? Ephesians 3:17 offers another source of sustenance.

4. The importance of good roots is undeniable. Jesus even referred to them in one of His parables. Matthew 13:6 is the snippet of the parable we want here, and Matthew 13:21 gives us the Lord's explanation of His tale. In the Parable of the Sower, what happens to the seeds that are thrown onto the rocks? Why?

*W*hen we moved into our most recent home, there were all of three trees in the yard—not nearly enough by our estimation. So every year we have added trees and shrubs around the property. Some came from cuttings we took from the trees at our old home—several willows and a few cottonwoods. Others were bought at the local nurseries—a paper birch, a flowering dogwood, three crepe myrtles, and a whole row of Bradford pear trees. With each addition, we watched and watered carefully. My five-year-old son offered to help with the watering duties. Clutching the hose in two hands, he would aim the nozzle high, sending a shower of rain across the baby tree's leaves. He needed to be taught it was the roots that needed the water more. A slow and steady trickle of water at the base of a tree does it much more good than a scatter of droplets across its leaves.

Are you getting nourishment from the Lord in erratic bursts that splash across your Sundays, or have you discovered the soul-satisfying nourishment of a steady supply from the Scriptures every day?

5. What happens to you when you face trials and temptations?

6. James mentions the message that God has planted in our hearts. What does he say about it in James 1:21?

Christ longs for us to experience a radical transformation of what comes naturally. Isn't that outlandish. All I can say is it's a good thing our God is big because, if we're going to be that different from our human nature, He's going to be very busy. Talk about a full-time job!

Patsy Clairmont

7. Paul uses planting as an illustration of his ministry. He went across the ancient world, sowing the seeds of the gospel everywhere he went. Paul didn't want Christians to give too much credit to his work, though. This is found in 1 Corinthians 3:6–7. What did Paul consider the most important ingredient in the nurturing of spiritual seeds?

8. Where are you planted? Where do you turn to find the spiritual nourishment you need? David offers some good words in Psalm 92:13.

9. Read Colossians 2:7. It is a prayer and an admonition for your life from Paul's pen.

✦ DIGGING DEEPER ✦

Several passages in the Bible speak of being rooted and of growing as we are given strength from God. Let's explore just a few here.

- Ezekiel 31:7
- Luke 6:44
- Romans 11:16, 18
- Colossians 2:19

✦ PONDER & PRAY ✦

Your study this week has provided seeds of thought and the watering of the Word. Ask the Lord to cause these seeds to grow, flourish, and blossom in your life. Pray for an excitement for deeper Bible study, and send out your roots deep into the Scriptures. Draw nourishment from the Living Word, and pray that "you will grow in faith, strong and vigorous in the truth" (Col. 2:7, NKJV).

✦ TRINKETS TO TREASURE ✦

Your trinket this week must be a tree—though it's hard to bring a maple or a scotch pine to every woman of faith in this study. So we shall content ourselves with a small tree, like the kind that dangles from the rearview mirrors of our cars. The tree shall remind you that "you shall be like a tree planted by rivers of water," able to weather storm and drought, only when your roots go down deep in Christ. Jesus is the source of your strength. Let your little pine tree be an invitation to read His Word, to do His will, and to bear fruit for His glory.

✦ Notes & Prayer Requests ✦

CHAPTER 4

WALK IN HIM

"AS YOU HAVE THEREFORE RECEIVED CHRIST JESUS THE LORD, SO WALK IN HIM"

Colossians 2:6, NKJV

Clever people can sell anything, even something that is free. Think about it. We buy bottled water. We buy cans of air. These salesmen are even selling us on one of our most basic activities—walking. Walking is good for us, so they say. Clever marketers have sold us walking shoes, coordinated walking outfits, pedometers, wristbands, water bottles, ankle weights, and even Walkman® radios. There are tapes to listen to while we walk away extra pounds. There are classes and videos to teach us proper walking techniques, all to promote putting one foot in front of the other!

Have you taken walking for granted? Unless we're confined for some reason or another, walking is how we get around. Without even thinking about it, we walk through malls, walk from office to office for meetings, or make our way through aisles of groceries. Walking comes as naturally as breathing or blinking. Most of us don't give it a second thought.

In the Bible, walking is equated with living. A person's walk involved their whole way of life. Just as our feet carry us into every situation of our days,

CLEARING
+ THE +
COBWEBS

Why is it easier to endure a long walk if you have someone to walk with?

so our "walk" involves every aspect of the business of living. Our walk with God is as basic as moving around on two feet. It should come as naturally as breathing, or blinking—or walking across the room.

1. Amos 3:3 reads like an ancient proverb: "Can two walk together, unless they are agreed?" That pretty much defines your relationship with God. You can't walk with Him unless you agree with Him. Read Deuteronomy 8:6 and 13:4. What did the Israelites understand "walking with God" to mean?

> *There's a safety factor in facing life's risks: Jesus. If you are walking toward Him to the best of your ability, He will see you through life's unpredictable waters— but you must risk launching the boat. Just ask Peter!*
>
> Patsy Clairmont

2. So many verses in the Bible speak of our walk with God. Each gives some little detail of *how* we should walk or *where* we should walk. Look up each of these Scripture passages and jot down a couple of words describing your walk with God.

- Psalm 26:11 _____   _____
- Psalm 86:11 _____   _____
- Psalm 119:35 _____   _____
- Ezekiel 20:19 _____   _____
- Micah 6:8_____   _____
- Romans 6:4 _____   _____
- Romans 8:1 _____   _____
- Romans 13:13 _____   _____
- 2 Corinthians 5:7 _____   _____
- Galatians 5:16 _____   _____
- Ephesians 5:2 _____   _____
- Ephesians 5:8 _____   _____

- Ephesians 5:15 _____   _____
- Colossians 4:5 _____   _____
- 1 Thessalonians 2:12 _____   _____
- 2 John 1:6 _____   _____
- 3 John 1:4 _____   _____

We don't start out being able to walk. It takes some time to get the hang of it. Have you ever watched a baby just learning to walk? It's so cute. She'll stand there, teetering on round little feet, trying desperately to balance herself. Then with arms outspread, she takes those first tottering steps. A smile spreads across her face, then *whump*, she'll land on her well-padded bottom. Unfazed by this temporary setback, and urged on by parental praise and encouragement, up she'll start again. These little ones are so determined to get things right. Persistently she'll practice, gaining confidence, steadiness, and speed. In a matter of weeks, the baby who was barely able to stand is running towards you across the floor!

Sometimes my spiritual walk reminds me of that toddler. I just get moving when something distracts me. Then, as soon as I turn my head to look off to the side, balance is lost and I land with an ungraceful *whump*. Keeping my focus straight ahead and keeping my life in balance can be a fulltime challenge.

3. Some of us are just beginning to toddle down the path God has prepared for us, while others are seasoned travelers who know enough to walk circumspectly. Either way, we all look to the Lord to point us in the right direction. How does David put it in Psalm 143:8?

If you need greater clarification in your life, if you're uncertain what next step you should take, if you long to make a difference in your world, then invite Christ to bring the light of His life into your darkened understanding. If you've done that and still feel as if you're stumbling around, then redouble your efforts to be in His light–bearing Word. Gather up His truth, store it in your heart, and then shine like crazy.

Patsy Clairmont

4. God's leading is trustworthy, for He has long known the paths we will travel. How does Paul describe us in Ephesians 2:10? In what path should we be walking?

5. Sometimes, as we go along through life, we notice the woman next to us. Her path is different than ours, and parts of it look prettier, or more exciting, or more restful. Jealousy creeps in, and we get miffed with God. How does Paul deal with these attitudes in 1 Corinthians 7:17?

Nothing in our lives is wasted. Not one thing that happens is without worth somewhere down the road. But we often miss it because we travel the beaten path and fail to open our eyes to the outlandish ways God wants to speak to us and love us and change us. We don't recognize the value in celebrating the strange twists, the difficulties, the so-called failures, when we really should . . . and could. We consider our flops or hard times a defeat, but in reality they are God's greatest compliments. They're transforming love gifts from a gracious heavenly Father.

Luci Swindoll

6. What is Paul's exhortation in Ephesians 4:1? What does it mean?

7. John knew Jesus very well. He was the "beloved disciple," and one of the three men who comprised Christ's inner circle of friends. John minces no words when he describes the Christian walk. What does he say in 1 John 2:6?

8. Last, let's look at a verse from Paul. What is his prayer for believers as found in Colossians 1:10?

> *It's easy to forget that we are called to bless God with our lives. We think that God is there to bless us; we think there should be some benefit to us at every moment. God does not exist just to make our lives better; we exist so that we can learn to love and worship Him in spirit and in truth.*
>
> Sheila Walsh

✦ DIGGING DEEPER ✦

Since this chapter has already sent you scampering through the pages of your Bible on a quest for "walking" verses, let's just share a couple of pretty word pictures from the Old Testament today. The first comes from God's own mouth. He has just chosen a man from among all the other men on the earth, and makes him many promises. He commands Abram, "Walk before Me" (Gen. 17:1). Decades later, near the end of his life, Abraham calls God "The Lord, before whom I walk" (Gen. 24:40). Through all the ups and downs of his life, Abraham learned that first lesson very well. He believed God, and is remembered for his faith even today.

✦ PONDER & PRAY ✦

Ask the Lord for insight this week as you consider your walk with Him. Are you moving forward, or have you been lured to a comfortable seat by the way? Pray for God's direction, then take to the path set before you with confidence. Ponder through the many verses you looked up in this chapter—words that describe your walk with the Lord. Pray that God would make these true statements about your own life in the weeks to come. May you walk worthy!

✦ TRINKETS TO TREASURE ✦

Walk in faith, walk in love, walk in wisdom, walk in truth! This week's gift is a reminder to keep on walking—new shoelaces! Use them to brighten up your own walking shoes. Every time you glance down and see their flash of color, let them recall Paul's urge to walk worthy of the One whose name you bear.

✦ Notes & Prayer Requests ✦

CHAPTER 5

TRUST IN HIM

"TRUST IN HIM AT ALL TIMES, YOU PEOPLE"

Psalm 62:8, NKJV

I have a son who is, to put it politely, *cautious*. He's been afraid of all the usual things—strangers, loud noises, new places, dark rooms, heights. When he was a baby, he screamed once at a bouncing ball. When it was time for him to graduate to the top bunk, he was afraid to climb the ladder. He wouldn't even consider entering the play place at our local McDonald's®, even after his younger brother began exploring its intricacies. He just wasn't ready, so I didn't push.

I remember a time when I tried to get him to go down a small slide at the playground at our church. It was really quite comical. I sat there, saying all the usual motherly things. "It's okay. It's not as scary as it looks. It's safe. See? Watch me do it. Come on, I'll help you. Don't you believe me? I'm right here. I'll catch you if you fall. Don't be afraid. I promise I'll be here." He would say that he believed me, but he just wouldn't go down that slide.

We are like that sometimes, when we face our difficulties. Jesus stands by our side, saying, "It's okay. It's not as scary as it looks. It's safe. See? Watch me do it. Come on, I'll help you. Don't you

CLEARING
✦ THE ✦
COBWEBS

Trust is really a fragile thing. Why is it so hard to trust someone again once they have lost your trust?

believe me? I'm right here. I'll catch you if you fall. Don't be afraid. I promise I'll be here." We say we believe Him, but we don't really trust Him. Do you trust in your Lord enough to put feet to your faith?

1. Paul gives a beautiful picture of the trust of a believer in Ephesians 1:13. What does he say there?

2. We say we trust Christ—that we believe in Him. What does *believe* mean? Is there a difference between believing that the sky is blue and believing in God?

> Human beings naturally become scared, angry, even ugly when they don't have control of what's going on in their lives. Even the most spiritually mature don't say, "Whatever, Lord!" without a few glitches now and then.
>
> Barbara Johnson

3. Paul says later that "the truth is in Jesus" (Eph. 4:21). That alone would make Him worthy of our trust, but it is even better than that. What does Jesus say in John 14:6?

4. What is proof of your trust in God? James offers a good illustration. Read James 2:22.

5. Faith without works is dead, to be sure. But remember that it is not the works that save us! We do what we do because we believe what God has said. What does God want us to do according to John 6:29?

> *When I am called to a behavior or attitude that is higher than my humanness, I'm comforted when I remember that it's not I, but He, who loves through me. Nevertheless, I need to get in concert with Him, and that means that my humanness must cooperate with His divineness.*
>
> Marilyn Meberg

The rope swing in our back yard was tied securely to a high branch in a towering old box elder tree. It was a long length of nylon rope, with a simple loop tied at the bottom. One foot could be placed in the loop, or you could simply sit on the knot. To make this amusement more exciting, my Dad propped an old ladder against one of the lower branches of the tree. My sister and I would take turns grabbing the loop of the rope swing, scampering up as high as we'd dare on the ladder, putting our foot in the loop, grabbing tight, and launching ourselves out into the air. Our confidence grew as time passed, and we became more daring. It was a long rope and a high ladder, so we were more than ten feet off the ground—my mother couldn't bear to watch us! With a rush of air and the creaking of the rope against the limb above us, we'd hang on until the swaying ride slowed to a halt. We used that rope swing daily. It was the centerpiece of our play.

I don't know if I could swing out on a rope swing anymore—so high, so fast. As a child, I trusted in my Dad's rope-tying abilities, I trusted the rope would hold me, I trusted that old tree branch to carry my weight, I trusted my ability to hang on for dear life. In fact, I trusted those things so much, that I never gave them a thought. No need to reason things through. No second-guessing or wondering why. Just grab on and jump! *That's* childlike faith.

> *Our impatience to have God move now, to act in ways that make sense to us, will drive us to take control of our lives. God is moving in ways that we cannot see or understand. This means we are left with the question, "Do I trust Him?"*
>
> Sheila Walsh

6. It is hardest to trust when we are confused and hurting. Life is filled with unexpected twists and turns we just don't understand. What does wise Solomon encourage us to do when we are unsettled? Look up Proverbs 3:5.

7. We have all been taught that if you want a job done right, you must do it yourself. Many of us would rather trust ourselves for direction in life—making our own plans and carrying them out. Trusting God means giving up that control. God is fond of the unexpected, and who knows what He might ask of us. We prefer predictability. Paul faced alarming circumstances. What does he write in 2 Corinthians 1:8–10? Why does He place His trust in God?

> *The road to glory is difficult with its rocks and boulders, its strain and struggle. But if you keep on keeping on, you can make it. Things aren't always as easy as we would like. Surprises and pitfalls wait for us along the road of life. We're going to sweat and sway, we're going to wonder why things are the way they are, and we're even going to blame other people. But every road has an end. If we can just hold on and keep climbing, knowing that God is aware of how we're straining, He will bring us up and over the mountains. It's consoling to know that God is in control of every part of our journey to glory, even over the steep mountains.*
>
> Thelma Wells

8. Why is God trustworthy? The Psalmist says "For You, Lord, have not forsaken those who seek You" (Ps. 9:10, NKJV). What promise has God made to secure your trust in Him? It's in Hebrews 13:5.

9. Jesus has made this same pledge. Look up Matthew 28:20.

10. And we have the Holy Spirit, as well. What does Jesus say about this Helper in John 16:7–15?

✦ DIGGING DEEPER ✦

God is trustworthy. God keeps His promises. God cannot lie. God will always be true to Himself. So we can trust Him! One of His promises to us throughout the Scriptures is the promise to never leave us nor forsake us. Let's look at several of the passages where He makes this promise to the faithful.

- Deuteronomy 31:6, 8
- Joshua 1:5
- 1 Kings 8:57
- 1 Chronicles 28:20
- Psalm 27:9

✦ PONDER & PRAY ✦

It is difficult to trust someone you don't know. God has promised He will be found by those who seek him (Jer. 29:13). Seek out the Lord this week, through His Word and through prayer. As you get to know Him better, and understand what He has promised, you will trust Him all the more. He will prove Himself to you again and again. Trust in Him!

✦ TRINKETS TO TREASURE ✦

You have heard the expression "Put your money where your mouth is!" It's a challenge of sorts. If you believe in something strongly—if you are certain you are right—then you should be willing to back what you say with cash. Now this doesn't necessarily mean placing bets and gambling. Investments would be a good example of putting money into something you trust. How about at church? You say you believe God's Word—does your offering each week back up what you claim? This week's trinket is meant to encourage you to "put your money where your mouth is"—to put feet to your faith. It's a penny, and if you look on that shiny copper coin you will see the words engraved right there: IN GOD WE TRUST.

✦ NOTES & PRAYER REQUESTS ✦

CHAPTER 6

COMPLETE IN HIM

"YOU ARE COMPLETE IN HIM"

Colossians 2:10

ell the truth. What's more fun—starting a new project, or finishing it? *Starting* one, of course! When I was a young girl, one of my aunts got me interested in counted cross-stitch. Thrilled at the prospect of creating something beautiful, I bought my first book of simple patterns and began making little Christmas ornaments. From there I moved on to jar lids, tiny wall hangings, and my first sampler. Projects quickly became more ambitious. Larger hoops were purchased, and my collection of embroidery floss expanded into two shoeboxes. Hours were spent each evening, quietly stitching in front of the television. It took patience and consistency to finish those large pieces.

Then I began subscribing to cross-stitch magazines, and borrowed pattern books from our library. My aunt would also lend me books, and I photocopied every project that I wanted to do. A growing excitement to start new patterns developed, and soon I had dozens of half-finished pieces piled on my bedroom shelves. It wasn't that I didn't *want* to finish the earlier pieces. It was just that the

CLEARING
✦ THE ✦
COBWEBS

How many unfinished projects are lying around your house—cross stitch samplers, scrap books, quilt tops, unsorted boxes of outgrown clothing, photo albums, filing, mending?

new pieces looked like so much more fun. Leaping into a new color scheme, a new pattern, a new look — it was thrilling.

So many things in life require time and patience to bring to completion. It's easy to become enamored of something new and something different. It's easy to become impatient with our lot and wish for something more exciting. Thank the Lord that God has the job of completing us. I'm not sure we'd stick with the job long enough to see it through!

1. I love the ends of Paul's letters. He crams in little bits of advice at the end, like a mother leaving for the weekend and calling out "Don't forget to feed the parakeet!" and "Don't use the good dishes!" One of Paul's parting shots to the church in Corinth was "Become complete" (2 Cor. 13:11). Do you feel complete?

As Christians, how often do we operate in the flesh and allow our jumbled thoughts and emotions to dictate our conduct? The fact is, when we take charge of a situation without consulting the wisdom of God, we always make a mess of it. Relationships get convoluted, hearts get broken, unfair and unkind words are spoken, egos are crushed, waves of doubt trouble us, distrust creeps in, guilt takes up residence, and emotions go haywire. Thangs ain't purty!

Thelma Wells

2. Most women look in the mirror and find something is lacking. If we were honest, we would admit the same is true when we look into our secret hearts. Where do you *usually* turn to feel more "put together"?

3. What has God promised you in Philippians 1:6?

4. This precious verse in Philippians holds a wonderful promise for us. Jesus will be faithful to complete the good work that He has begun in us. However, there is the flip-side. Pretend you are a pessimist for just a minute. What else does this verse mean?

5. According to James 1:2–4, what is the mark of completion in a believer—what makes her perfect?

6. Have you heard the old proverb, "The road to hell is paved with good intentions." It is dangerous to have only excitement and good intentions about obeying God. What does Paul urge the church at Corinth in 2 Corinthians 8:11?

> *A cartoon I saw recently showed a couple in a car coming upon a road sign reading, "Highway of Life. Construction Zone Next Forty Years." Isn't that just how it is— constant changes, detours, something being built as something else is being torn down? Life is never a done deal; it's never perfect. And it will never be perfect in this broken, mixed-up world. There isn't a perfect anything. The perfect picture hasn't been painted, the perfect poem hasn't been written, and the perfect song hasn't been sung. Everything in the world remains to be done over and done better.*
>
> Barbara Johnson

*S*tarting fresh feels good. We can erase last week's failures and begin again. Nearly every week I resolve to exercise daily, drink more water, eat more vegetables, and ignore my sweet tooth. That happens on Monday, and by Wednesday I am getting edgy. By Thursday I am shamelessly rummaging around in the cupboards for chocolate chips.

Each one of us needs a new beginning at some point or another. But it needn't come with a bang of fireworks or a streaking comet. New beginnings often come slowly. They may even sneak up on you— like a tiny ray of sun slipping out from beneath a black cloud. You can be inspired by the smallest things, so keep your eyes open.

Barbara Johnson

True resolve, a commitment to my decision, a dedication to follow my own rules—any of these things would help carry me through when temptation strikes. A little patience and determination would help me complete one week of healthy habits—and then another and another.

Don't get me wrong, I realize God is the God of second chances. His willingness to forgive our shortcomings is vast. His love is boundless. His mercy is right there for the asking. But forward progress in our walk with God won't come without some resolve, dedication, and sacrifice on our part. Completion—maturity—can only come with patience and commitment.

7. In one of Paul's letters, he includes a greeting from one of his friends. The message Epaphras passes along through Paul is that he's been praying for those back home. What was his prayer for them? It's in Colossians 4:12.

I think we Christians have become lazy. We would rather read a book about how someone else became closer to God than spend time alone with Him ourselves. We would rather listen to someone else's interpretation of the Word of God than read it for ourselves. And yet we alone are accountable for what we believe. We can't stand before God on the Day of Judgment and explain that our incredible ignorance is our pastor's fault. It is our responsibility to access God's Word for ourselves.

Sheila Walsh

8. What does the writer of Hebrews pray for Christians in Hebrews 13:21?

9. So, here's what we know: completion is better than good intentions, our completion is underway, we can pray for one another's completion, and if we have patience, we are well on our way to being complete. If that still seems a little vague, let us look at one more passage. Paul, in his last words to his beloved son in the faith, Timothy, gives him the *secret* to becoming complete. Read 2 Timothy 3:1–17.

✦ DIGGING DEEPER ✦

Since the "secret" to being complete in Christ is the Bible, let's look at a few verses from the Scriptures that speak directly about the Word of God.

- Luke 4:4
- Luke 11:28
- Romans 10:17
- Ephesians 6:17
- Hebrews 4:12
- Revelation 19:13

✦ PONDER & PRAY ✦

Sit down with God this week and look over some of your good intentions. Is there something you feel He would like you to bring to completion this year? Pray it through, make your plans, then forge ahead! Take Paul's last words to Timothy to heart this week. Your Bible is God's divine message to you. By exploring its pages, you will learn to know Him better. You will discover what brings Him pleasure, what glorifies His name, and what He longs to give you. God will use His Word to bring along to completion that good work He has begun in you.

✦ TRINKETS TO TREASURE ✦

This week's trinket is a reminder not to pave your road in life with a bunch of good intentions. It's a little paver—a tile. God's goal for your life is for you to be complete in Him. He asks you to devote yourself, to have patience, and to move towards maturity. You are His masterpiece and you *will* be complete someday. Pave your path—not with mere intentions—but with prayer, gifts of service, moral integrity, love for fellow believers, compassion for the hurting, commitment to God's Word, the fruit of the Spirit, unshakeable faith, and all the other things God calls us to in the Scriptures.

✦ NOTES & PRAYER REQUESTS ✦

CHAPTER 7

STRONG IN HIM

"BE STRONG IN THE LORD AND IN THE POWER OF HIS MIGHT."

Ephesians 6:10, NKJV

D o you ever wonder how the saints who have gone before feel about having their lives recorded in the Bible? At first you might think, "Wow! I'd love that!" People would read about you for centuries after you were gone. Mothers would name their babies after you. Preachers would use you as an illustration in their Sunday sermons. You'd have your own little figure on those flannel graph boards. People discuss how they can't wait to meet you in heaven. Chuck Swindoll might write a whole book about your life of faith.

But then it dawns on you. You won't get to approve the final manuscript, and God might include some pretty embarrassing things in your life story. Sure, many ancient believers are members of the Bible's "Hall of Faith." But consider the character traits of these nominees for the Bible's "Hall of Weakness."

Eve was a blame-shifter. Cain let anger and bitterness turn to hatred and murder. Noah had a weakness for wine. Abraham told lies to protect himself. Sarah was jealous of a younger woman. Rebekah played favorites with her children. Jacob

CLEARING
+ THE +
COBWEBS

Anyone who doubts a woman's capacity for strength hasn't experienced childbirth! Here's your chance, girl! Tell us your "war story"—how many hours, how many pounds?

was sly. Rachel was envious of her sister's successes. Moses was afraid to speak in public. Aaron succumbed to peer pressure. Samson was a womanizer. David tried to hide the evidence of his sins. Peter tended to speak before thinking. Thomas placed facts before faith. Ananias and Sapphira were greedy. Martha let busyness distract her from the Lord. Euodia and Syntyche let petty differences come between them. Onesimus tried to run away from his responsibilities.

Yet if you look at the end of the "Hall of Faith" in Hebrews 11, you will find a little phrase in the midst the volleys of praise. The writer states that these faithful men and women "out of weakness were made strong" (Heb. 11:34). So you see, they weren't so very different from us after all!

1. Does physical strength guarantee a measure of moral fortitude?

2. On the other hand, does physical weakness also sap our inner strength and faith?

3. We *are* weak. Some of us are physically weak. I love the passage in Hebrews that prays, "strengthen the hands which hang down and the feeble knees" (Heb 12:12). *All* of us are spiritually weak—don't try to deny it. Even the pillar of faith, Paul, admitted to this. What does Romans 7:18 say?

4. Paul encourages his fellow believers to "stand fast in the faith, be brave, be strong" (1 Cor. 16:13). Yet he is vulnerable enough to admit his own weaknesses. What does he say in 2 Corinthians 12:10?

5. What does that mean—"when I am weak, then I am strong"? The verse beforehand helps us out a bit. Read 2 Corinthians 12:9. What does God say?

> *Each of us has something broken in our lives: a broken promise, a broken dream, a broken marriage, a broken heart . . . and we must decide how we're going to deal with our brokenness. We can wallow in self-pity or regret, accomplishing nothing and having no fun or joy in our circumstances; or we can determine with our will to take a few risks, get out of our comfort zone, and see what God will do to bring unexpected delight in our time of need.*
>
> Luci Swindoll

*S*trength is such a manly quality. It's hard for a lady to wrap her arms around a description like "tough as nails" or "strong as an ox." No woman wants to be compared to an ox! Though most of us are not "mighty oaks," we do possess God-given strengths. We would just word them a little differently.

How about "strong as Aunt Edna's coffee" or "steady as a pair of orthopedic shoes." Maybe you are as strong as superhold hairspray or as durable as name-brand paper towels. Many women face sacrifice and service daily. Nobody notices their steadiness. No one admires them for their dedication. There is a quiet strength in women that enables them to do the thing that is in front of them. The strength you have may be small, but serve your Lord with all the strength you have. Give it all you've got!

6. God strengthens us, and asks us to give that strength back to Him. For what are you relying on the Lord's strength to accomplish this week?

Lord, help me not to look for an easy way out like a child seeking recess or a toddler searching for her pacifier. Help me to take responsibility before you and others for my actions and reactions. Thank you that I can choose to give up my childishness and instead experience childlike joy.

Patsy Clairmont

7. God likes surprises. What does He do, according to 1 Corinthians 1:27?

8. Here's a familiar verse with a familiar promise—Philippians 4:13. Do you believe it?

Be brave. Then braver still. Never resist His insistence on your perfection. He is working all things together for good, not just for you and yours, but for people you've never met and may not meet until your paths cross in heaven.

Barbara Johnson

9. Here's a sweet benediction prayer from Peter. He prayed for believers to be strong in the Lord. Read it in 1 Peter 5:10. What does he mention comes before that strength? But then what comes at the end?

✦ DIGGING DEEPER ✦

Consider Jesus' Words in Mark 12:33: "One must love God with all his heart, all his mind, and all his strength" (NCV). What areas of your life would fall into the "with all your strength" portion of that command?

✦ PONDER & PRAY ✦

This week, when you find yourself at your weakest—suffering from a headache, short on sleep, disappointed, irritable, and coming into *that* time of the month—pray fervently for God's strength. He can give you the grace to carry on normally in spite of your personal struggles. During those times when you feel completely useless, He may just surprise you by using you mightily. So trust God to uphold you, and be strong in Him.

✦ TRINKETS TO TREASURE ✦

This week's trinket will be a reminder of both strength and fragility— an egg. We know how fragile they are. Special cartons have been created to keep them safe, and eggs are always bagged separately at the grocery store and placed in the seat of the cart next to our purses. Eggs should come with little labels that say "fragile" and "handle with care." But scientists also tell us that eggs were designed by God to be amazingly sturdy. They protect the growing baby within, and can withstand the bumps and jostles that come their way. Though your strength may seem as fragile as an eggshell, know that you are made perfect in your weakness. Be strong in Him!

✦ Notes & Prayer Requests ✦

CHAPTER 8

REJOICE IN HIM

"REJOICE IN THE LORD ALWAYS. AGAIN I WILL SAY, REJOICE!"

Philippians 4:4, NKJV

Have you ever been to a bridal shower or a baby shower? Most of us have. It's a chance to shower a new bride or mother-to-be with gifts to help them through the new season of life they are entering. Showers are a chance to dust off the punch bowl and make fussy foods. Pastel colors reign in the decorations, and a table stands ready to receive the mountain of presents.

The mainstay of the traditional shower, however, has to be the silly games we all play. We create bride's gowns from toilet paper. We sift through bowls of rice while blindfolded, looking for tiny gold safety pins. We force the bride-to-be to bake a cake from scratch without a recipe. We write cute messages on newborn-size diapers. We unscramble nursery rhymes. We match up famous couples throughout history. We make a relay race out of diaper changing and sorting socks. Showers are a chance to rejoice with the rejoicing.

One part of the shower ceremonies always left me stumped though. At most of these events, the hostess will pass out index cards and pencils and

---

CLEARING
✦ THE ✦
COBWEBS

Do you have a favorite praise chorus? What is it about that particular song that speaks to your heart?

say something like, "Write down your advice to the new mom" or "Impart some wisdom from your vast experience to this new bride." A daunting task. It would be easier to say something silly, but I really wanted to say something helpful. Then, a few years back, I hit upon my tidbit of advice. I have given it freely since then, and I share it with you. Sing around the house. Whether you are a new bride, just starting out, or a new mother, welcoming a little person into your home, fill that home with the sounds of rejoicing. Sing! It will lift your heart into the heavens even as your hands are busy about the tasks of home.

1. Paul says believers should be "speaking to one another in psalms and hymns and spiritual songs, singing and making melody in your heart to the Lord" (Eph. 5:19, NKJV). How do you show those around you that your heart is filled with rejoicing?

Whiners neither enjoy nor give joy. But grace-filled people are reputable, sought after, and deeply loved. They stand heads above others even while on their knees. They are full of forgiveness and wisdom. You often find them nurturing children, caring for the ill, serving the underprivileged, applauding the successes of others, and celebrating God's generosity.

Patsy Clairmont

2. Our thankful hearts overflow with praise. How does David describe our rejoicing in Psalm 33:1?

3. Why do we rejoice? In the midst of everyday life or in spite of deep heartache, what reason do we have for joy? What does Luke 10:20 say?

4. David says we shall rejoice "because we have trusted in His holy name" (Ps. 33:21, NKJV). Our trust in Jesus has also given us access to joy. Why do we have reason to rejoice according to Romans 5:2?

*ave you ever had one of those weeks? The car keys are nowhere to be found. You were stuck in rush hour traffic for over an hour three times this week already. The in-laws called out of the blue to let you know they're dropping by on their way to Florida. You have been out of dog food for two days. A raccoon scattered your garbage across three yards last night. The kids have come down with stomach flu. You get a flat tire. You suddenly realize it was your sister's birthday yesterday. There's a run in your pantyhose. Your check to the electric company bounced and they're threatening to cut your power. The baby must be teething again. You've just discovered that your garage leaks. Your son's piano recital and your daughter's softball game are scheduled for the same afternoon. And your husband suddenly decides he wants to buy a boat.

> We are going to inherit the new heaven and the new earth. If we could see now all God has planned for us, we'd be beside ourselves with anticipation and joy. We'd be going around with an unquenchable grin on our faces and a boisterous song in our hearts. Not deceived by pain, we'd be absolutely certain of our future. Our lives would inspire exciting headlines rather than dull platitudes.
>
> Barbara Johnson

We really do have weeks when we feel overloaded by life. Too much is happening, and our sanity is under strain. Those are the times when it is hard to maintain a thankful attitude. Those are the days when it's hard to rejoice. But those are the days when joy is most needed!

5. When should we rejoice? 1 Thessalonians 5:16 gives a straightforward reply.

6. There are times when we must rejoice "even though." Joy in the midst of hardship is a gift from God. Paul understood this when he wrote, "I now rejoice in my sufferings for you" (Col. 1:24). Peter also encouraged believers to face suffering with joy. What does he say in 1 Peter 4:13?

7. Jesus promised His grief-stricken disciples a return of joy. What are His words in John 16:22? They can truly apply to us, as well.

> Belonging to Jesus Christ means that you've been given a heart transplant. With a new heart, He gives the power to be joyful, exuberant, and thankful. Eternal values replace temporary ones.
>
> Barbara Johnson

8. We did not walk with Jesus as His disciples did, yet we love Him. Peter, who did walk at Jesus' side gives encouragement to all of us, who came to faith afterwards. What does he say in 1 Peter 1:8?

9. *Love* is a word that can be both a noun and a verb. For example, when used as a verb, we can say "I will love you forever," but when used as a noun we would say "My love is like a red, red rose." You see? *Joy* is generally used as a noun, like "the joy of the Lord is my strength." However there is a verse that uses joy as a verb. Look up Habakkuk 3:18.

> *How often have I looked outside myself for peace and joy and intimacy in my relationship with Christ, as if it were a gift that someone else might give me? We think that if we read the right book or attend the right conference or travel to the church where everyone is saying that God is showing up in unprecedented ways, then we will find that wonder—that joy—we are seeking.*
>
> Sheila Walsh

✦ DIGGING DEEPER ✦

We are given joy. We are commanded to rejoice. We, above all, have reason to rejoice. The Scriptures are rich with words of praise and reasons to rejoice. Let's look at just a few of them.

- Psalm 97:12
- Isaiah 61:10
- Romans 12:15
- 1 Corinthians 13:6
- Philippians 2:16

✦ PONDER & PRAY ✦

Choose a favorite old hymn out of a hymnal this week and memorize *all* the verses. Since this will require a lot of practice, sing while you do the dishes, sing while you fold the laundry, sing while you take a shower, and sing while you are driving in the car. Pray that the Lord will fill your heart with thankfulness this week that will spill out in joyful praise—*even* when things don't go all that smoothly.

✦ TRINKETS TO TREASURE ✦

Your small treasure this week is a pocket calendar. Before you is a whole year, more than three hundred days. And each of those days holds the promise of joy for you. Certainly you don't know what those days ahead might bring. But rejoicing in Christ—rejoicing *always*—means that every one of those dates has been reserved for rejoicing.

✦ NOTES & PRAYER REQUESTS ✦

_____

_____

_____

_____

_____

_____

_____

_____

_____

CHAPTER 9

REFRESHED IN HIM

"LET ME HAVE JOY FROM YOU IN THE LORD; REFRESH MY HEART IN THE LORD"

Philemon 1:20, NKJV

Didn't you just hate naptime when you were a kid? And don't you just love naps now? It's really too bad we didn't appreciate them back when we had time to take them! Children who are resisting sleep are not too hard to spot in a crowd. If they are young enough, they still try pulling their ears and tugging at their hair in an effort to stay awake. Older, more savvy children have laid aside such obvious ploys in favor of constant motion. The more tired the child, the wilder their activity. When you finally get them cornered, it's funny to see them drop. Even in the face of sheer exhaustion, they try to deny the obvious. It's hard to say whether mother or child is more relieved when that tousled head hits the pillow.

Even as adults, we need rest and refreshment from time to time. Jesus found time to draw away from the crowds and have quiet times with His Father. We need to follow His example, and turn to the Lord for refreshment.

CLEARING ✦ THE ✦ COBWEBS

As far as I'm concerned, nothing beats a Sunday afternoon nap! How do you usually spend your "day of rest"?

1. God invented weekends—sort of. He *did* set apart a day of rest for His people, and no working was allowed. Why does Jesus say that the day was created? It's in Mark 2:27.

> Christ is enough for all of us. His mercy helps us to see others mercifully, and His loving acceptance of us enables us to accept ourselves and others. With that as a beginning point, we can relax, be ourselves, and come out from behind the protective walls we've erected. Then we can connect with others who have discovered the joy of just being themselves.
>
> Sheila Walsh

2. Rest and refreshment were always offered to travelers in Bible times. What were Abraham's words in Genesis 18:5 to the men who were passing by?

3. Jesus offers the believer refreshment. What does He say in John 6:51, 58? And what does He say He will give in John 4:10–14?

4. Jesus is the head of the Church. How does He care for us according to Ephesians 5:29?

reshness is a valued quality these days. Women want to smell fresh, feel fresh, and be fresh-faced. We use phrases like "fresh as a daisy" and "let me just freshen up a bit." Advertisers have latched onto this idea, and try to infuse their products with appeal by saying they're fresh. "Clean and refreshing!" "Minty fresh!" "Fresh as a mountain breeze!" We buy air fresheners and breath fresheners. We equate freshness with lemonade, peppermint candy, morning air, iced tea, waterfalls, and swimming pools.

Whether it's looking at your life through fresh eyes, gaining a fresh perspective, or taking a refresher course, every Christian needs to be refreshed sometimes. God's Word offers daily refreshment for our souls. God's people can refresh our hearts by their love and encouragement. Rest in the Lord. Refresh your Christian sisters!

5. We are called upon to uphold and encourage one another within the church. To this end, Christians have been given gifts. Why, according to Ephesians 4:11–12?

Many blessings have been given to me: More joy than I ever imagined having, more love than I ever dreamed I'd know, more encouragement than I deserve. But I know God didn't bless me with these gifts so I could sit back in the recliner and keep them all to myself.

Barbara Johnson

6. What is the foundation of edification? Paul mentions it in 1 Corinthians 8:1.

7. God's care refreshes our souls. He loves us uncondi- tionally, even when we are being difficult to love. This is important to keep in mind when we reach out in love to those around us. How does Peter put it in 1 Peter 4:8?

8. When you are weary, burned out, stumbling, and just plain tuckered out, God can lift you up. He will refresh your spirit if only you ask Him. What familiar words do we find in Isaiah 40:31?

9. When we sin, we suddenly find ourselves out of step with God. Shame, remorse, and contrition fill us. We want to be on our guard next time, steadfast against stumbling over that same weakness again. How does David put it in Psalm 51:10?

10. Jesus knew we would face hardships and burdens in our lives. In Matthew 11:28, He offers each of us a precious invitation. What is it?

> *It behooves us all to extend a hand to the sister who slips and slides her way past us in life. She needs us. And before very much time passes, we'll need her.*
>
> Marilyn Meberg

✦ DIGGING DEEPER ✦

Back in the "old days," churches would change the pace of their services and bring in a special speaker. There would be a different face in the pulpit, and a fresh message from God's Word. People's excitement for the Lord would be renewed, and a firm dedication and resolve to walk worthy would be made. These were called revival meetings. Many churches still hold them regularly. Revival and refreshment go hand in hand, so let's explore some verses that speak of revival today (NKJV).

- Psalm 80:18
- Psalm 85:6
- Psalm 119:37
- Psalm 143:11
- Isaiah 57:15

✦ PONDER & PRAY ✦

As you turn to the Lord for the refreshment of your soul this week, ask Him for inspiration. He can put the most wonderful ideas into your head to uplift, encourage, and refresh those around you. Ask God to deepen your love so that it will cover a multitude of sins. Don't simply revel in the refreshment and renewal of your spirit. Let it flow through you into the lives of those around you. Once you are refreshed in Him, be a joy-bringer!

✦ TRINKETS TO TREASURE ✦

Your reminder to be refreshed in Christ is a package of breath fresheners. A mint is a small thing, but it freshens the breath, soothes a dry throat, and wakes a person up a bit when their attention wanders. Every time you pop one in your mouth, and you experience that minty fresh feeling, call to mind Jesus' words. He alone has offered to revive your weary soul in such a way that you will never hunger or thirst again. Jesus has promised to nourish and cherish His church, and He invites us to come to Him with our burdens. And remember too, that mints are meant to be shared. Look for ways to encourage and refresh those around you.

✦ NOTES & PRAYER REQUESTS ✦

CHAPTER 10

BOLD IN HIM

"I HAVE NOT KEPT THIS GOOD NEWS HIDDEN IN MY HEART; I HAVE TALKED ABOUT YOUR FAITHFULNESS AND SAVING POWER. I HAVE TOLD EVERYONE IN THE GREAT ASSEMBLY OF YOUR UNFAILING LOVE AND FAITHFULNESS."

Psalm 40:10, NLT

When I was growing up, there were two different rooms in our house that had very similar furnishings. They both held couches and chairs. They both had lamps and books. They both had scenes painted on the walls and pretty curtains. But they were very different.

The first of these two rooms was the living room. The carpet was beige, the couch and chairs were upholstered in neutral colors. The curtains were light and airy. The scene my mother had painted on the wall was of wispy birches. It was a beautiful room, and children were not allowed to play in it. You walked through the living room on tiptoe. You did not bounce on the couch. You did not move the pillows. This room was "for good," and no toys ever found their way into this quiet domain.

On the other hand, there was the family room. The carpet was a multicolored shag and the couch

CLEARING ✦ THE ✦ COBWEBS

Was there something in your house when you were growing up that was "untouchable"— something your parents didn't want you to play with or touch? What was it?

a sturdy brown color. A child-sized kitchen stood against one wall, and a toy box in the corner. The wall was painted with giant sunflowers, and the television set was always tuned in for *Sesame Street* and *The Electric Company*. My sister and I spent hours playing in the family room every day.

Before Jesus came, getting close to God was like tiptoeing into the living room. Only the High Priest entered the Holy of Holies, and only on special occasions. When Jesus died for our sins, the great curtain that hid the inner sanctuary was torn in two. Now, believers can go boldly before the throne of God because of Jesus' sacrifice. We're part of God's family now, and welcomed into the family room. Though we probably shouldn't jump on the furniture, metaphorically speaking of course, we are welcomed before the throne of grace. We can spend hours there every day in prayer.

1. Jesus called His Father "Abba," the equivalent of "Daddy" in His language (Mark 14:36). He invited believers to join Him in calling God our Father. What does Jesus declare in Matthew 12:50?

> *God is interested in the tiniest things in the world. He cares about us and what we consider important. He gives us the desires of our hearts. He completes what He begins. He knows us by name.*
>
> Luci Swindoll

2. With what attitude can we now turn to the Heavenly Father? Both Ephesians 3:12 and Hebrews 10:19 make this clear.

3. Often "bold" is used in a negative sense, speaking of the brash and disrespectful. What is meant by "bold" here, and why can we have such boldness?

4. Boldness in approaching the Father is not often a problem for believers. We long for a comfortable, familiar relationship with our God. But sharing our faith with others can leave us tongue-tied and red-cheeked. What is your experience in speaking about the things of the Lord?

> *To be in Christ is to live a life that is anything but a cliché. Watch out! God is making you authentic. Real. Rubbing off your fake fur. Changing your outlook. Giving you new desires. Making you marvelous. Fulfilling what you were created for. He is making you the "Queen of Quite a Lot," enlightening you for kingdom work.*
>
> Barbara Johnson

5. Confidence comes with two things. First of all, in order to tell others about Jesus, you must know of what you speak. What does Peter encourage in 1 Peter 3:15?

6. So understanding *what* we believe can give us confidence to share those beliefs. That was our first step towards boldness. The other factor that brings confidence is . . . practice. What does Jesus tell us to do in Matthew 10:27?

> *That's the mystery of the gift of grace. It shows up just when you need it. Not a moment too soon, but not a moment too late.*
>
> Sheila Walsh

*S*o you cannot give some great theological treatise. So you cannot read Greek or Hebrew. So you don't know your "isms" from your "ologies." So what! Very few of us will ever be great orators. Not everyone is prepared to debate the finer points of doctrine. And that's okay.

God uses the simple things of the world to confound the wise. In other words, He can take our everyday routines, our ordinary circumstances, and our simple faith to change lives. I love the old adage, "Bloom where you're planted." Don't let fears and uncertainties get in the way of showing God's love. Reach out to those around you. Tell them about your own experiences. God will use your kindness and unselfishness to capture the attention of the lonely and lost. The Spirit will kindle their hearts to know this same peace and joy you possess. Be matter of fact about God's love, grace, and forgiveness. And relax. You can't mess up eternity for them. We can just share from our hearts. Only the Spirit can change theirs!

7. When facing a friend who does not know the Lord, it's often difficult to nudge the conversation into spiritual things. All those verses you memorized seem to disappear right along with any boldness. What does Paul mention as a good starting point for the sharing of one's faith? Read Philemon 1:6.

Being touched by God's extravagant grace ignites something within us that causes others to notice. It's an interior glow that is like an exterior light in that it casts its influence in spite of the degree of darkness in which it finds itself— not only in spite of the darkness but also because of it. In the darkness the light becomes more attractive, more influential, more valuable, and more obvious.

Patsy Clairmont

8. Everyone gets nervous, even the apostles. So do what they did, and pray for boldness. Ask others to pray for you. What is the prayer of Acts 4:29?

9. God has not called you to hide your little light under a bushel basket. Live in such a way to make others notice a difference. Tell others about Him. What does Paul say in 2 Corinthians 2:14 about sharing what we know of the Savior?

✦ DIGGING DEEPER ✦

The call to courage can be found throughout the Scriptures. Here are several passages from the Bible where boldness is indispensable:

- Psalm 138:3
- 2 Corinthians 3:12
- 1 Thessalonians 2:2
- Proverbs 28:1
- Philippians 1:14, 20
- 1 John 4:17

✦ PONDER & PRAY ✦

You can be bold in Christ! Take advantage of your welcome at the throne of God to commit this week to prayer. Let an attitude of prayer become a familiar feeling. Go to God again and again until you are comfortable in His presence. Rest in Him, relax in His presence, and tell Him everything that's on your mind. You are His child, and He loves to hear your voice.

✦ Trinkets to Treasure ✦

This week's trinket is a reminder to be bold in Christ—bold as brass. It's a brass button. Whenever the shine catches your eye, remember that you can boldly go where no one has gone before. You have been invited into God's very throne room, where your prayers are welcomed and heard. Then, you must be bold as brass to share your faith with your friends and family who are not believers. Be prepared to explain your faith, and be willing to tell people how Jesus has touched your life.

✦ Notes & Prayer Requests ✦

_____

_____

_____

_____

_____

_____

_____

_____

_____

CHAPTER 11

HOPE IN HIM

"THE LORD JESUS CHRIST, OUR HOPE."

1 Timothy 1:1, NKJV

hristians understand that Jesus is coming back. We've been waiting for Him for a very long time. We call Him our soon-coming King. Our pastors tell us His return is imminent—it could happen at any time. We are called to watchfulness, to earnest expectation. *This* could be the day! Such messages have always stirred my heart. It all sounds really exciting. But days, months, and years have passed, and still no trumpet blast. Decades and centuries have marched on by, and still no mighty shout. We're rather in the habit of Jesus *not* coming, and so His return has lost some of its imminency.

However, I have had a handful of very thorough lessons on the imminence of a coming. To be sure, so have you, if you are a mother. There isn't a woman who's endured the ninth month of pregnancy who doesn't understand what imminence is! The ninth month is spent longing for the baby's arrival. It's on the forefront of every expectant mother's mind. The first thought as our heads hit the pillow each night is "I wonder if it will be tonight?" The first thought that enters our

CLEARING
✦ THE ✦
COBWEBS

In a way, hope is having something to look forward to. What are the kinds of things you hope for?

minds every morning is "I wonder if it will be today?" We know it will be soon. We long for delivery.

Do you long for Jesus' return? Is your greatest hope in Him?

1. Christians are the only people on this planet with true hope—a living hope, according to 1 Peter 1:3. We say our hope is in Jesus Christ. What exactly is it that we are hoping for? Look in Titus 1:2.

2. Many generations have passed since Jesus walked this earth. Believers in every one of those generations carried the same hope we now hold. Do you think they were disappointed not to see Jesus' return in their lifetime? Why or why not? Romans 5:5 gives us a hint.

> When I think of the way eager anticipation has ended in disappointing reality so many times in my life, I'm thankful to remember that there's one place I can anticipate going to that will be even better than I expect. I can't even imagine all the wonderful things that are waiting for me there. And I know my home is there, prepared for me, grander than anything on earth, because God Himself told me so.
>
> Barbara Johnson

3. We have probably all memorized Hebrews 11:1 at some point in our lives: "Now faith is the substance of things hoped for, the evidence of things not seen" (NKJV). Faith and hope are intertwined. Look at Romans 8:24–25. What attitude does hope create in our hearts?

4. So if we are hoping in something we cannot see, and we have no idea when this hope might come to pass, what is the basis of our hope? How do we even know what to hope for? Let's turn to Romans again — Romans 15:4.

> *We have not even begun to see what God has in store for us. Even the best moments that He showers on us are hardly the appetizer for the banquet He has prepared. Hold on to your hats, girls, we've only just begun to experience all the delights God has prepared for us.*
>
> Sheila Walsh

5. What was Paul's greatest hope? He tells us in 1 Thessalonians 2:19.

*D*id you have a hope chest when you were a teenager? They were all the rage several decades ago. Every girl had one. Hope chests were a throwback to the days when a girl must have a dowry in order to marry. In more recent times, they were more of a practicality. As a girl learned the skills of sewing and homemaking, she began to set aside certain items for her hope chest. Embroidered pillowcases, lace doilies, quilts, rugs, some of grandmother's recipes, and a precious teacup or two. No bride came empty-handed into her new home. Over her years of preparation, she would set aside beautiful things for the future home she hoped to have. Even before she was engaged to be married, she was laying aside little treasures that she would use later.

   In a way, heaven is our hope chest, for we can lay aside treasures there, where they cannot be destroyed. Are you making preparations for eternity? Is your treasure in heaven?

6. How do these New Testament passages describe our hope in Christ?

Romans 12:12

Colossians 1:27

1 Thessalonians 1:3

1 Thessalonians 5:8

1 Timothy 1:1

Titus 1:2

Hebrews 6:19

Hebrews 10:23

7. We can cherish hope, even in seemingly impossible situations. The story of Abraham's life is a prime example of such unshakeable hope. How is Abraham described in Romans 4:18?

8. Believers can carry their hope in the face of anything they encounter, even the bleakest of circumstances. What does Paul encourage believers to remember in 1 Thess. 4:13–14?

9. Paul's benedictions—his closing prayers—are some of the most beautiful portions of the New Testament. Read his benediction of hope in Romans 15:13. What has the God of hope given you?

In every situation, whether ordinary or life threatening, God assures us that He keeps His eyes on us and knows the number of hairs on our heads. Absolutely everything that can happen to us—good, bad, or indifferent—God knows and cares about. God is concerned about us all the time, in every area of our lives, even if nobody else is. He promises that we are never away from His presence.

Thelma Wells

✦ DIGGING DEEPER ✦

We hope in Christ for eternal life. What do the Scriptures say about the eternity ahead of us? Let's look at just a few verses that speak about the life we have been promised.

- Romans 6:23
- 1 Timothy 6:12
- Titus 3:7
- 1 John 2:25
- 1 John 5:11
- Jude 1:21

✦ PONDER & PRAY ✦

Why not memorize Paul's benediction of hope this week: "May the God of hope fill you with all joy and peace in believing, that you may abound in hope by the power of the Holy Spirit" (Rom. 15:13, NKJV). It is a prayer of promise, indeed! Hold onto your hope, and thank the Lord for His faithfulness in fulfilling His promises to you. No matter what, you can hope in Him.

✦ TRINKETS TO TREASURE ✦

This week's treasure is a tiny hope chest, to remind you of all that awaits you. Jesus has given you many gifts—forgiveness, peace with God, and the hope of eternal life. Someday, we shall join all the other believers, from every generation, tribe, and nation. We will spend eternity with our Creator, our Savior. Until then, we can hang onto our hope. Let this little box—this hope chest—remind you of where your future lies.

✦ Notes & Prayer Requests ✦

CHAPTER 12

GLORY IN HIM

"HE WHO GLORIES, LET HIM GLORY IN THE LORD."

1 Corinthians 1:31, NKJV

Whenever my husband and I break out the board games, there can be trouble. It's not that I don't enjoy playing—I love all sorts of games. Scrabble®, Scatergories®, Hugger Mugger®, Boggle®, Taboo®, Balderdash®, Mad Gab®, Pictionary®,—*word* games. I'm good with words, and I often win, so word games are fun! Strategy games are my downfall. In checkers, I worry more about the patterns the checkers make on the board than the game. In chess, I'm making up stories about the playing pieces. In Monopoly®, I'd trade Marvin Gardens and Ventnor for Baltic, just because I like purple better than yellow. If my husband talks me into a game of Risk®, I take his bids for world domination personally. (I always end up in tears.) Why can't he just let my little armies live in peace? I run into trouble with these games because I tend to miss the point of the game. My choices don't line up with the objectives of the games. I'm choosing favorite colors instead of making sound business decisions. I'm avoiding conflict when I should be going on the offensive.

Sometimes Christians live life like it is a game. We enjoy moving our tokens around in circles,

CLEARING
✦ THE ✦
COBWEBS

Is there something you do regularly that you feel your family or friends take for granted? Is there something God does regularly for you that you take for granted?

making deals, earning money, having fun. But that's not why we're here. The Bible tells us our purpose, the whole point of our existence, is to bring glory to God. Do your choices line up with that objective for living? Have you made that the basis for your way of life? Or are you missing the point?

1. Who shall glory in the Lord? David tells us in Psalm 86:9.

> The events of our lives, when we let God use them, become the mysterious and perfect preparation for the work He has called us to. The truth is that our trials are a furnace forging us into gold.
>
> Barbara Johnson

2. We were created to bring glory to God. Even Jesus, during His lifetime here on earth, was most concerned in bringing glory to His Father. What does John record in John 12:28 and John 13:32?

3. That was then, and this is now. Where shall God be glorified today?

4. God will be glorified by the church as a whole, but our own individual lives can bring glory to His name, too. What does Paul urge in 1 Corinthians 6:20?

5. No matter what happens in your life, God can be glorified as a result. For instance, if you are rescued, God will be glorified. What does Psalm 50:15 say?

6. If you suffer, God will be glorified. What does it say in 1 Peter 4:16?

We sing about God's glory all the time in church. "To God be the glory, great things He hath done." "Glorify Thy name in all the earth." "All glory, laud, and honor, to Thee Redeemer, King." "In my life Lord, be glorified." "To God be the glory for the things He has done" (My Tribute). "We will glorify the King of kings; we will glorify the Lamb. We will glorify the Lord of lords; who is the great I Am."

Songs of praise are one way to glorify God. They are certainly not the only way.

7. How can we bring glory to God? Jesus commands one way in Matthew 5:16.

> *We look for spiritual moments in places where we think they should occur, as we gather to worship or as we kneel in prayer, but sometimes we are gifted—when it seems as if the Lord graciously allows His glory to visit our kitchen. Savor that moment and rest in Him.*
>
> Sheila Walsh

8. Can you think of other ways in which your life can bring glory to God? Consider carefully, and list a few here.

9. Lift up your voice with David's as you read Psalm 86:12. How does he wish to glorify God?

✦ DIGGING DEEPER ✦

This week, instead of exploring your Bible for verses on glorifying God, I want you to borrow a hymnal. Have you ever read through the words of hymns before? They can be an incredible source of inspiration and encouragement. They are filled with some of our most basic beliefs. And, they will get you humming. Search out your favorite hymns this week, and sing them to your Savior.

✦ PONDER & PRAY ✦

Pray this week for God to help you see the point. Ask Him to show you how you can bring glory to His name in your life. God may not ask you to do earth-shattering feats. He may just be asking you to do your everyday tasks faithfully. Follow His lead as the Spirit prompts you — His nudging is unmistakable. And in whatever you do, acknowledge God, giving Him the glory He is due. Glory in Him.

✦ TRINKETS TO TREASURE ✦

All of God's creation brings Him glory. The angels declare before the throne of God, "The whole earth is full of His glory" (Is. 6:3, NKJV). The Psalmist says, "The heavens declare the glory of God; And the firmament shows His handiwork" (Ps. 19:1, NKJV). For this week's trinket, you shall have a star. Hang it up in your bedroom, and watch for its glow when bedtime rolls around. May it remind you of your objective — to bring glory to God — just like the twinkling stars in the night sky.

✦ NOTES & PRAYER REQUESTS ✦

✦ SHALL WE REVIEW? ✦

Every chapter has added a new trinket to your treasure trove of memories. Let's remind ourselves of the lessons they hold for us!

1. An ivy cutting

A snippet of something alive to bring to mind your new life in Christ. A life that will flourish and grow. A life that can be shared with others by allowing Christ to live through you.

2. A glass bauble

One of Barbara Johnson's "splashes of joy" for you to tuck away in a hidden place. It is to remind you to decorate the hidden places of your heart with a quiet and gentle spirit.

3. A tree

We are to be like trees, planted by rivers of water. Our roots must go down deep into Christ's love and teaching.

4. A shoelace

A reminder to lace up and keep walking in Christ. We are called to walk worthy of the One whose name we bear.

5. A penny

Like the engraving on the coin, we must declare that "in God we trust." We believe His Word, we trust in His faithfulness, and so we are willing to "put our money where our mouth is."

6. A tile

Here is our reminder not to pave our lives with a bunch of good intentions. We are God's masterpiece, and He has promised that we will be complete in Him.

7. An egg

Though we may feel as weak and fragile as an eggshell, God has promised His strength will be made perfect through us. We can be strong in Him.

8. A pocket calendar

We cannot know what all the days ahead of us will hold, but every one of those days has been reserved for rejoicing. Rejoice in Christ—always!

9. A breath freshener

A burst of minty freshness to remind you that Christ offers you refreshment from your burdens. He can renew your strength and revive your weary soul. In turn, we can offer refreshment and encouragement to one another.

10. A brass button

Because of Christ's sacrifice we can be bold—bold as brass. We have been invited into God's very throne room, where our prayers are welcomed and heard.

11. A hope chest

A reminder of the hope we have in Jesus—hope for forgiveness, for His return, and for eternal life.

12. A glowing star

The heavens declare the glory of God, and so must we. The purpose of our lives is to glorify God—just like the twinkling stars in the night sky.

✦ LEADER'S GUIDE ✦

Chapter 1

1. "God the Lord, Who created the heavens and stretched them out, Who spread forth the earth and that which comes from it, Who gives breath to the people on it, And spirit to those who walk on it" (Job 33:4, NKJV). God created us, giving us both the breath of life and an eternal spirit.

2. "You He made alive, who were dead in trespasses and sins" (Eph. 2:1, NKJV). Though we are alive, we were dead. All of us were born sinners. Our black little hearts were obvious to our parents from the start. We've always needed God's mercy and grace.

3. "God has given us eternal life, and this life is in His Son" (1 John 5:11, NKJV). Believers are promised eternity with Him. Our life here on earth is just the beginning.

4. "For you have been born again. Your new life did not come from your earthly parents because the life they gave you will end in death. But this new life will last forever because it comes from the eternal, living word of God" (1 Pet. 1:23, NLT). Unless Jesus returns within our lifetimes, we will surely die. That's just a fact of life. However, eternity is a promise we can hold on to. This new life we have begun here on earth will last forever.

5. "Those who receive His new life will no longer live to please themselves. Instead they will live to please Christ, who died and was raised for them" (2 Cor. 5:15, NLT). Christians are new people. The old life is gone. A new life begins. We have a change of heart. New priorities are in place. We make our choices with God's approval in mind. We live to please Him.

6. "Since Christ lives within you, even though your body will die because of sin, your spirit is alive because you have been made right with God" (Rom. 8:10, NLT). This verse is where we get that old phrase, being "right with God."

7. "Since you have been raised to new life with Christ, set your sights on the realities of heaven, where Christ sits at God's right hand in the place of honor and power" (Col. 3:1, NKJV). Paul urges His Christian brothers and sisters to change their perspective. Where this world and its concerns once filled their minds, they should now set their sights on the reality of heaven. Once they had self-centered goals, schemes, and wish lists, but now they have glimpsed the bigger picture.

8. "I have been crucified with Christ; it is no longer I who live, but Christ lives in me; and the life which I now live in the flesh I live by faith in the Son of God" (Gal. 2:20, NKJV). The life we now live is not our own. We owe our life to Jesus, and so we live out our days in gratitude for His sacrifice. He should be our first thought—His plans, His ways, His responses, His compassion, His priorities, His glory.

9. Did you know that Jesus said, "Anyone who believes in Me will do the same works I have done, and even greater works" (John 14:12, NLT)? He wasn't saying that His followers would do more impressive things than He had done—you can't outshine God! No, He was talking about scope. We can do more for the kingdom because there are more of us doing His work. So get out there and share the life you now have!

10. "Some people, by always continuing to do good, live for God's glory, for honor, and for life that has no end. God will give them life forever" (Rom. 2:7, NCV). Eternity is our reward, but while we're waiting for heaven, there are things we can be doing. Those who are faithful are described as living for God's glory, honoring Him, and always doing good. Such a life is the mark of a true Christian.

Chapter 2

1. There are times in everyone's life when we don't think we can face the thing in front of us. We would rather turn and hide. For some of us it is on-the-job frustrations. For some it is the constant clamor of children. For some of us it is worry over finances. For some of us it is an incurable illness or the loss of a loved one.

2. "I will say to the Lord, 'You are my place of safety and protection. You are my God and I trust You'" (Ps. 91:2, NCV). David shouts with joy, he sings of God's power, he trusts in His unfailing love. "For You have been my refuge, a place of safety in the day of distress" (Ps. 59:16, NLT).

3. Before ascending into heaven, returning to His Father, Jesus gives these last words of encouragement and admonition, "Teach them to obey everything that I have taught you, and I will be with you always, even until the end of this age" (Matt. 28:20, NCV). Jesus is always near to us. He has promised to be with us no matter what we go through.

4. "There is no creature hidden from His sight" (Heb. 4:13, NKJV). Our loving Heavenly Father doesn't miss a thing, and no one can snatch us out of His care. Life is hard, and bad things sometimes happen, but those of us who belong to God are hidden in Him forever.

5. Jesus prayed to His Father, "I am leaving them behind and coming to You. Holy Father, keep them and care for them—all those You have given Me . . . I'm not asking You to take them out of the world, but to keep them safe from the evil one. They are not part of this world any more than I am" (John 17:11–16, NLT). Jesus prayed for His friends just like we do, asking God to hide them in His hand and protect them along the way.

6. "In Him lie hidden all the treasures of wisdom and knowledge" (Col. 2:3, NLT). Paul tells Christians this so they will remember where to turn when they are confused. By this time, copies of the Gospels were being circulated, and they had access to the teachings of Jesus. All around them are people who have convincing arguments for their own way of believing, but the church at Colosse are encouraged to remain strong in their faith. In verse six, Paul says "And now, just as you accepted Christ Jesus as your Lord, you must continue to live in obedience to Him" (Col. 2:6, NLT). Everything we need is hidden in Christ.

7. Peter is speaking of a woman's beauty when he says "let it be the hidden person of the heart, with the incorruptible beauty of a gentle and quiet spirit, which is very precious in the sight of God" (1 Pet. 3:4, NKJV). Women are not to put all their emphasis on good grooming. Care must be taken to maintain an inner beauty as well. Remember, what is hidden inside will always come out—be careful what you harbor in your heart.

8. "Your Word I have hidden in my heart, that I might not sin against You" (Ps. 119:11, NKJV). If you are troubled by bad thoughts or bad memories, combat those impulses with God's Word. Replace them with memorized Scriptures. Fill your mind with the Bible's promises, and darkness will be driven away.

9. "Behold, You desire truth in the inward parts, and in the hidden part You will make me to know wisdom" (Ps. 51:6, NKJV). When we are hiding God's truth in our hearts, God will show us His wisdom. If you long for wisdom from God, this verse is a good place to start.

10. "Store your treasures in heaven, where they will never become moth-eaten or rusty and where they will be safe from thieves" (Matt. 6:20, NLT). And in Luke: "The purses of heaven have no holes in them. Your treasure will be safe—no thief can steal it and no moth can destroy it" (Luke 12:33, NLT).

Chapter 3

1. "He shall be like a tree planted by the waters, which spreads out its roots by the river" (Jer. 17:8, NKJV). Though the trees in these verses face heat and drought, they thrive. Their leaves remain green and they bring a bountiful harvest because their roots have a constant source of water. Their location, firmly planted by the source of their strength, ensures their prosperity.

2. "Rooted and built up in Him and established in the faith, as you have been taught, abounding in it with thanksgiving" (Col. 2:7, NKJV). Christians do indeed depend upon Christ as their source. Paul says that we're to be established in the faith, and that we will have a bounteous harvest of thanksgiving.

3. "You, being rooted and grounded in love" (Eph. 3:17, NKJV). I especially like this verse in the New Living Translation, for it reads, "I pray that Christ will be more and more at home in your hearts as you trust Him. May your roots go down deep into the soil of God's marvelous love." Does Jesus feel right at home with you? Do your roots run deep into God's love, drawing strength and confidence from His marvelous love for you?

4. "When the sun came up, it burned the young plants; and because the roots had not grown deep enough, the plants soon dried up" (Matt. 13:6, TEV). Luke gives us another glimpse of Jesus' explanation of His parable: "The ones on the rock are those who, when they hear, receive the word with joy; and these have no root, who believe for a while and in time of temptation fall away" (Luke 8:13, NKJV).

5. Do you read the Lord's Words with joy in your heart on Sundays, only to stumble and fall by Tuesday? When you face trying circumstances, draw strength from your roots. God will supply you with the grace, the love, the strength, and the peace to stand the heat and weather the drought. Keep drawing from His supply!

6. "So get rid of every filthy habit and all wicked conduct. Submit to God and accept the word He plants in your hearts, which is able to save you" (James 1:21, TEV). God's Word is able to save you, and in order to truly submit to it, believers are asked to rid themselves of old ways. Thankfully, God is able to do this work in our hearts. It happens even as we seek Him in His Word.

7. "I planted the seed, and Apollos watered it. But God is the One who made it grow. So the one who plants is not important, and the one who waters is not important. Only God, who makes things grow, is important" (1 Cor. 3:6–7, NCV). We can witness, we can pray, we can reason, and we can teach, but only God can change a person's heart. God uses all of our efforts, but in the end, He is the One who nurtures a believer's soul.

8. "Those who are planted in the house of the Lord shall flourish in the courts of our God" (Ps. 92:13, NKJV). Do you have a special spot in the house where you go to read and pray? Do you have a radio program that you regularly tune into to find Bible teaching? Does your pastor speak the Word on Sundays? Are you involved in a Bible study or prayer group? Send out those roots, and draw it all in.

9. "Let your roots grow down into him and draw up nourishment from him, so you will grow in faith, strong and vigorous in the truth you were taught. Let your lives overflow with thanksgiving for all he has done" (Col. 2:7, NLT).

Chapter 4

1. "Keep the commandments of the Lord your God," "fear Him," "obey His voice," "serve Him," and "hold fast to Him" (Deut. 8:6; 13:4). Walking involved trust, belief, obedience, and proper reverence. It still does!

2. Here are the descriptions of our walk with God from each verse:
Psalm 26:11, walk in integrity
Psalm 86:11, walk in truth
Psalm 119:35, walk in God's commandments
Ezekiel 20:19, walk in God's statutes
Micah 6:8, walk humbly
Romans 6:4, walk in newness of life
Romans 8:1, walk according to the Spirit
Romans 13:13, walk properly
2 Corinthians 5:7, walk by faith
Galatians 5:16, walk in the Spirit
Ephesians 5:2, walk in love
Ephesians 5:8, walk as children of light
Ephesians 5:15, walk circumspectly
Colossians 4:5, walk in wisdom
1 Thessalonians 2:12, walk worthy of God
2 John 1:6, walk according to His commandments
3 John 1:4, walk in the truth

3. "Cause me to hear Your lovingkindness in the morning, for in You do I trust; cause me to know the way in which I should walk, for I lift up my soul to You" (Ps. 143:8, NKJV). Morning is a good time to ask the Lord to guide us through our day. He gives wisdom to those who ask, and will open our eyes to see the needs around us. We can trust His promptings.

4. "We are His workmanship, created in Christ Jesus for good works, which God prepared beforehand that we should walk in them" (Eph. 2:10, NKJV). In another translation, this verse states that we are God's masterpiece. Great care went into our making. Paul says in Ephesians that God has created us for good works — to do good as we walk.

5. There's no room for sibling rivalry in God's family. Each of us is a one-of-a-kind creation. Each of us has a different personality, unique gifts, opportunities, and callings. Paul says, "As God has distributed to each one, as the Lord has called each one, so let him walk" (1 Cor. 7:17, NKJV). Live for God right where you are!

6. "Walk worthy of the calling with which you were called" (Eph. 4:1, NKJV). Walking worthy of your calling means living in such a way that lives up to the One whose name you bear. As Christians, our walk should be worthy of Jesus Himself.

7. "He who says he abides in Him ought himself also to walk just as He walked" (1 John 2:6, NKJV). This is the verse that inspired such books as *In His Steps* and such fads as W.W.J.D. bracelets.

8. "That you may walk worthy of the Lord, fully pleasing Him, being fruitful in every good work and increasing in the knowledge of God" (Col. 1:10, NKJV). That is my prayer for you as well, sister.

Chapter 5

1. "In Him you also trusted, after you heard the word of truth, the gospel of your salvation; in whom also, having believed, you were sealed with the Holy Spirit of promise" (Eph. 1:13, NKJV). We were told about Jesus, His sacrifice, and His gift of salvation. We believed!

2. We all affirm that the sky is blue. It is a fact, and we agree that it is so. Many people say that they believe there is a God. But saying there is a God is not enough to save one's soul. Even the demons and the devil can confirm this fact — and they are all doomed (James 2:19). The belief we are called to is not mental assent. We are called to believe in such a way that it affects our actions. If we *really* believe what Jesus Christ has said, we *must* change in order to obey. It's like that old hymn "Trust and Obey" — believing is trusting *and* obedience!

3. "I am the way, the truth, and the life. No one comes to the Father except through Me" (John 14:6, NKJV). In fact, Jesus *is* the truth.

4. "You see, he was trusting God so much that he was willing to do whatever God told him to do. His faith was made complete by what he did—by his actions" (James 2:22, NLT). Faith is the starting point, but follow-through is vital. Your actions are proof of what you believe. Your trust is made complete when you act upon it.

5. John 6:29 says "The work God wants you to do is this: Believe the One He sent." God wants believers to *believe* Him. Believing God is not simply understanding things with your head. Faith is not just a fact-finding tour. Knowledge is a starting point, but it cannot be the stopping point. James says that to believe God's commandments and yet not act upon them is a sure sign of a dead faith (James 2:17). Jesus says "if you love Me, keep My commandments" (Matt. 15:10). Believe Jesus, and let what you believe transform your life. Live out your faith.

6. "Trust in the Lord with all your heart, and lean not on your own understanding" (Prov. 3:5, NKJV). There will be times when all we can do is trust God. We don't understand what we're going through or why, but we've given our hearts to the Lord. We will lean on Him.

7. "We were crushed and completely overwhelmed, and we thought we would never live through it. In fact, we expected to die. But as a result, we learned not to rely on ourselves, but on God who can raise the dead. And He did deliver us from mortal danger. And we are confident that He will continue to deliver us" (2 Cor. 1:8-10, NLT). God can rescue us from the scariest situations. And even if we face death, we can rely on Him because He can raise us up!

8. "For He Himself has said, 'I will never leave you nor forsake you'" (Heb. 13:5, NKJV). God has promised to always be by your side, and God cannot lie! He will be there for you.

9. "Lo, I am with you always, even to the end of the age" (Matt. 28:20, NKJV). No matter where we are, or when we are, Jesus is with us.

10. "I tell you the truth. It is to your advantage that I go away; for if I do not go away, the Helper will not come to you; but if I depart, I will send Him to you" (John 16:7, NKJV). Jesus promised that having the Spirit with us would be even better than if He were to stick around—"it is to your advantage." So now, we believers have the Spirit always with us. God the Father has promised to be with us. Jesus has promised to be with us. And the Spirit is always with us—within us in fact.

Chapter 6

1. Oh my! You didn't need to shout "no" quite so loudly! Though we may be the most self-assured of women, we know that deep down inside something is lacking, missing, unfinished, off kilter—incomplete.

2. Many of us had hoped our husbands would complete us. Some of us thought that becoming a mother would fill that mysterious gap. We try to fill that incompleteness with church activities, education, community service, and successful careers. Most of us have tried little self-improvements: new shoes, painted nails, a cute little top, an exercise class, highlighted hair, tweezed eyebrows. We may come out looking good, but only God can touch that empty spot we try so hard to fill.

3. "God began doing a good work in you, and I am sure He will continue it until it is finished when Jesus Christ comes again" (Phil. 1:6, NCV). You are a "good work" in process, and God has promised to complete His work in you.

4. You got it. This verse also points out that the work of completion will not be done anytime soon. What has been begun will be under heavy construction until Jesus returns. Nobody will achieve perfection on this earth.

5. "Let your patience show itself perfectly in what you do. Then you will be perfect and complete and will have everything you need" (James 1:4, NCV). Patience. Once patience is allowed to work in us and on us, we will lack nothing.

6. "Now you should carry this project through to completion just as enthusiastically as you began it" (2 Cor. 8:11, NLT). Though planning and anticipation are half the fun of any task, nothing gets done unless somebody does it. What plans have you made for the Lord lately—regular quiet times, praying for missionaries, Scripture memorization, family devotions, extra giving to your church, prayer walks, Bible study, morning and evening prayers, journaling, backyard Bible clubs? Has your readiness to desire these things brought about a completion?

7. "Epaphras, who is one of you, a bondservant of Christ, greets you, always laboring fervently for you in prayers, that you may stand perfect and complete in all the will of God" (Col. 4:12, NKJV). Pray for your sisters, that they might be complete in Him.

8. "Now may the God of peace . . . make you complete in every good work to do His will, working in you what is well pleasing in His sight, through Jesus Christ, to whom be glory forever and ever. Amen" (Heb. 13:18, 21, NKJV). Completion involves doing good works, doing God's will, pleasing God, and glorifying Jesus Christ.

9. "All Scripture is given by inspiration of God, and is profitable for doctrine, for reproof, for correction, for instruction in righteousness, that the man of God may be complete, thoroughly equipped for every good work" (2 Tim. 3:16–17, NKJV). There you have it folks. You absolutely cannot become a complete Christian without your Bible. Read it daily. Memorize it. Study it. Meditate on its words. Pray through it. Do what God says. It is the living Word of God, and it will change you from the inside out. That's the only "secret" there is.

Chapter 7

1. Of course not. Samson would be a good example of this. Though God gifted him with tremendous physical strength, he proved to be a man with many weaknesses. Samson was disobedient, stubborn, selfish, vengeful, lustful, petty, and easily manipulated.

2. Remember the old proverb "The spirit is willing but the flesh is weak." Though our faith may be strong, our bodies may be weak, crippled, and aging. The woman with an issue of blood in the gospels would be a good example of faith in the midst of pain and weakness. Though drained by years of illness, she had the courage to pursue the Lord and the faith to be healed.

3. "I know I am rotten through and through so far as my old sinful nature is concerned. No matter which way I turn, I can't make myself do right. I want to, but I can't" (Rom. 7:18, NLT).

4. "For this reason I am happy when I have weaknesses, insults, hard times, sufferings, and all kinds of troubles for Christ. Because when I am weak, then I am truly strong" (2 Cor. 12:10, NCV).

5. "And He said to me, 'My grace is sufficient for you, for My strength is made perfect in weakness.' Therefore most gladly I will rather boast in my infirmities, that the power of Christ may rest upon me" (2 Cor. 12:9, NKJV).

6. It takes the Lord's own miraculous strength to survive some days—putting up with difficult coworkers, dealing calmly with independent teens, listening patiently to small children's chatter, answering the same question *again*, waiting in line at the slowest register, running late, running short, running out.

7. "God purposely chose what the world considers nonsense in order to shame the wise, and he chose what the world considers weak in order to shame the powerful" (1 Cor. 1:27, TEV). God uses the weak to astonish those who think they are wise. He is fond of using the unexpected.

8. "I can do all things through Christ who strengthens me" (Phil. 4:13, NKJV). All means all. Jesus will support you, and His strength will never run out.

9. "May the God of all grace . . . after you have suffered a while, perfect, establish, strengthen, and settle you" (1 Pet. 5:10, NKJV). Peter points out that there will be suffering in this world, but in the end, God will strengthen and settle us.

Chapter 8

1. Singing, dancing, skipping, whistling, humming, smiling, laughing, crying, praising, shouting, sharing, hugging.

2. "Rejoice in the Lord, O you righteous! For praise from the upright is beautiful" (Ps. 33:1, NKJV). The psalmist even says that God inhabits our praise (Ps. 22:3, KJV), or as the New King James says, He is enthroned by praise. How lovely.

3. Rejoice because your names are written in heaven" (Luke 10:20, NKJV). Did you know that when you meet the Lord in heaven, He will give you a new name? After all, there will probably be millions of Jenny's in heaven, and zillions of Mary's. He will give you a name all your own (Rev. 2:17).

4. "Because of our faith, Christ has brought us into this place of highest privilege where we now stand, and we confidently and joyfully look forward to sharing God's glory" (Rom. 5:2, NLT). We not only have the assurance of a right relationship with God here and now, but we have the joy of heaven to look forward to.

5. "Rejoice always" (1 Thess. 5:16, NKJV).

6. "Rejoice to the extent that you partake of Christ's sufferings, that when His glory is revealed, you may also be glad with exceeding joy" (1 Pet. 4:13, NKJV). The Bible is very matter of fact about suffering and pain. They are a part of our lives in this fallen world. The people Peter was writing to were faced with a difficult choice—either to hide their convictions, pretending to fit into their society, or to suffer and even die for their faith. Peter assures them that choosing to suffer for a short time here will only intensify their joy in eternity.

7. "You now have sorrow, but I will see you again and your heart will rejoice, and your joy no one will take from you" (John 16:22, NKJV). Someday, perhaps one day soon, we will have no need for tears. Then we will have joy that will never leave.

8. "You have not seen Christ, but still you love him. You cannot see him now, but you believe in him. So you are filled with a joy that cannot be explained, a joy full of glory" (1 Pet. 1:8, NCV). This echoes what Jesus told Thomas: "Jesus said to him, 'Thomas because you have seen Me, you have believed. Blessed are those who have not seen and yet have believed'" (John 20:29, NKJV). We have faith in unseen things, and it is a source of great joy.

9. "I will rejoice in the Lord, I will joy in the God of my salvation" (Hab. 3:18, NKJV).

Chapter 9

1. "The Sabbath was made for man, and not man for the Sabbath" (Mark 2:27, NKJV). The Pharisees had built up so many rules around the Sabbath that it was a chore not to break one of them. God intended for the last day of the week to be a respite from daily labors. It was to be a holy day, set apart for God.

2. "I will bring a morsel of bread, that you may refresh your hearts" (Gen. 18:5, NKJV). As it turns out, that "morsel of bread" became a lavish little feast, and the guests turned out to be angels! Don't you just love the invitation to "refresh your hearts"?

3. Jesus says, "I am the living bread which came down from heaven. If anyone eats of this bread, he will live forever" (John 6:51, NKJV) and "whoever drinks the water I give will never be thirsty" (John 4:14, NCV). He sustains us spiritually just as food and drink keep our bodies alive. Without Him, we would be spiritually dead.

4. Jesus "nourishes and cherishes" the Church, according to the New King James Version. Just think—He cherishes each one of us, and nourishes us spiritually. Other translations will say "feeds and takes care of" (NCV) or "lovingly cares for" (NLT). When you are feeling worn out, Jesus can refresh your spirit.

5. "For the equipping of the saints for the work of ministry, for the edifying of the body of Christ" (Eph. 4:12, NKJV). The gifts are our equipment. They enable us to serve one another, and to edify the church.

6. "Knowledge puffs up, but love edifies." The foundation of edification is in love.

7. "Most important of all, continue to show deep love for each other, for love covers a multitude of sins" (1 Pet. 4:8, NKJV). This is especially important to remember when dealing with those closest to us. When we know a husband, a friend, or a child so well, their little quirks and idiosyncrasies can really start to annoy us. They can begin to get on our nerves, make us short tempered, and overthrow our kindness. Choose instead to love wholeheartedly. Let your love for them run deep, and forgive folks for their little oddities.

8. "Those who wait on the Lord shall renew their strength; they shall mount up with wings like eagles, they shall run and not be weary, they shall walk and not faint" (Is. 40:31, NKJV). Wait on the Lord, and He will strengthen you. Not only will you be able to walk again, He will make you fly.

9. "Create in me a clean heart, O God. And renew a steadfast spirit within me" (Ps. 51:10, NKJV). When the Lord forgives us, we have the elation of a renewed right relationship. God can give us a renewed resolve to walk rightly—a steadfast spirit.

10. "Come to Me, all you who labor and are heavy laden, and I will give you rest" (Matt. 11:28, NKJV). Rest, relief, refreshment, revival, renewal—they can all be found in Him.

Chapter 10

1. "Whoever does the will of My Father in heaven is My brother and sister and mother" (Matt. 12:50, NKJV). Believers are adopted right into the family. Jesus invites us to call God our Father as well.

2. "Because of Christ and our faith in Him, we can now come fearlessly into God's presence, assured of His glad welcome" (Eph. 3:12, NLT). We can boldly approach our Heavenly Father because we know that we are welcomed because of Jesus.

3. The dictionary defines *bold* as "fearless and daring; exhibiting courage and bravery." When we are told to approach our Heavenly Father with boldness, it is an invitation to come to God without fear. In the past, God was unapproachable, hidden from view by a thick veil. Only the High Priest could enter God's presence, and only once a year. He did so after much preparation and with great fear and trembling. In fact, priests did their duties with bells jingling at their hemline and a rope tied around their ankles. This was a precaution against an outpouring of God's wrath. Should the bells fall silent, the priests waiting outside were prepared to drag a stricken priest out of the Holies with the rope. We can now have boldness in approaching the Father, for our sins are forgiven and we are welcomed as adopted sons and daughters.

4. Dry mouth? Muddled thoughts? Sudden uncertainties? All of us have dreaded trying to steer a conversation into the right direction to mention our personal faith in Jesus. We have inhibitions, experience awkwardness, and get cold feet. Perhaps it would settle our stomachs and calm our hearts to remember that nothing we say or do will *make* our friend become a Christian. We can share from our hearts, but only the Spirit can change him/her.

5. "Always be ready to give a defense to everyone who asks you a reason for the hope that is in you" (1 Pet. 3:15, NKJV). Do what it takes to really grasp the essence of the gospel. Study the "Roman Road" or write it all out. The only way to "be ready" is to prepare yourself. But remember—even when you go into certain situations feeling ill prepared to take a stand, God can give you the words to speak. Remember what Jesus said in Matthew 10:19? "Do not worry about how or what you should speak. For it will be given to you in that hour what you should speak" (NKJV). Don't be afraid.

6. "What I am telling you in the dark you must repeat in broad daylight, and what you have heard in private you must announce from the housetops" (Matt. 10:27, TEV). Jesus says to tell the world, so do it—make it your practice. And practice makes perfect, so they say.

7. "The sharing of your faith may become effective by the acknowledgement of every good thing which is in you in Christ Jesus" (Philem. 1:6, NKJV). Little stories from your everyday experiences are easy to share. They can become opportunities to tell your friends about how God has touched you.

8. "Now Lord, look on their threats, and grant to Your servants that with all boldness they may speak Your word" (Acts 4:29, NKJV).

9. "Now thanks be to God who always leads us in triumph in Christ, and through us diffuses the fragrance of His knowledge in every place" (2 Cor. 2:14, NKJV). People learn of Him through us *and* God will always lead us into triumph. Victory is assured. So be bold!

Chapter 11

1. "In hope of eternal life which God, who cannot lie, promised before time began" (Titus 1:2, NKJV). Our hope lies in the return of Jesus Christ and in our resurrection to eternal life with Him.

2. "Now hope does not disappoint, because the love of God has been poured out in our hearts by the Holy Spirit who was given to us" (Rom. 5:5, NKJV). We cannot become hopeless in waiting because all the while we are experiencing the love of God and the presence of His Spirit.

3. "For we were saved in this hope, but hope that is seen is not hope; for why does one still hope for what he sees? But if we hope for what we do not see, we eagerly wait for it with perseverance" (Rom. 8:24–25, NKJV). Because we hope for Christ's return, we face each day with eager anticipation. We persevere in saying to ourselves, "Perhaps today."

4. "Everything written in the Scriptures was written to teach us, in order that we might have hope through the patience and encouragement which the Scriptures give us" (Rom. 15:4, TEV). The Bible is our source of understanding. God's promises give us our hope. Jesus' own words give us the encouragement to persevere.

5. "After all, what gives us hope and joy, and what is our proud reward and crown? It is you! Yes, you will bring us much joy as we stand together before our Lord Jesus when he comes back again" (1 Thess. 2:19, NLT). Paul found great joy in leading people to Jesus and salvation. His hope in Christ's return was paired with the expectation of a joyful reunion with all the men and women he had ministered to and with.

6. Here are the various descriptions of our hope in Christ:
Romans 12:12, hope causes us to rejoice
Colossians 1:27, we hope for glory
1 Thessalonians 1:3, our hope is patient
1 Thessalonians 5:8, we wear our hope of salvation like a helmet
1 Timothy 1:1, Jesus Christ is our hope
Titus 1:2, we hope for eternal life
Hebrews 6:19, this hope is an anchor for our souls
Hebrews 10:23, our hope is unwavering

7. "Who, contrary to hope, in hope believed, so that he became the father of many nations" (Rom. 4:18, NKJV). Abraham was willing to take a true leap of faith and believe God's outrageous promises. Though God's promise of a son seemed hopeless, Abraham grabbed hold, and "in hope believed." We, too, can have such faith.

8. Have you heard the saying, "While there is life, there is hope"? Well, Christians have hope even in the face of death. Paul says "I do not want you to be ignorant, brethren, concerning those who have fallen asleep, lest you sorrow as others who have no hope. For if we believe that Jesus died and rose again, even so God will bring with Him those who sleep in Jesus" (1 Thess. 4:13–14, NKJV). We have hope in God's promise that we will see our beloved Christian brothers and sisters again someday. Even death cannot drive hope away.

9. "Now may the God of hope fill you with all joy and peace in believing, that you may abound in hope by the power of the Holy Spirit" (Rom. 15:13, NKJV). You will have joy. You will have peace. And your hope will multiply!

Chapter 12

1. "All nations whom You have made shall come and worship before You, O Lord, and shall glorify Your name" (Ps. 86:9, NKJV). The Lord created the entire world, and all the world will glorify Him.

2. "'Father, glorify Your name.' Then a voice came from heaven, saying. 'I have both glorified it and will glorify it again'" (John 12:28, NKJV). "If God receives glory through him, then God will give glory to the Son through himself. And God will give him glory quickly" (John 13:32, NCV).

3. "To Him be glory in the church by Christ Jesus to all generations" (Eph. 3:21, NKJV). We who are believers can bring glory to God's name in our lives.

4. "For you were bought at a price; therefore glorify God in your body and in your spirit, which are God's" (1 Cor. 6:20, NKJV). Paul put it this way: "We are the first people who hoped in Christ, and we were chosen so that we would bring praise to God's glory" (Eph. 1:12, NCV).

5. "Call upon Me in the day of trouble; I will deliver you, and you shall glorify Me" (Ps. 50:15, NKJV). The praise that flows from a thankful heart will bring God glory. He is also glorified every time we tell the story of our deliverance.

6. "If anyone suffers as a Christian, let him not be ashamed, but let him glorify God in this matter" (1 Pet. 4:16, NKJV). Those who refuse to deny their Lord in the face of harsh persecution, and stand up for their faith, draw attention to God. Anyone who is willing to die for what she believes makes people think. Anyone who is willing to live for what she believes is a beacon that points to Christ.

7. "Let your light so shine before men, that they may see your good works and glorify your Father in heaven" (Matt. 5:16, NKJV). What we do and how we live will turn heads. If we are faithful, God will be glorified.

8. Cheerful obedience, calm acceptance, selflessness, compassion, patience, forgiveness, consideration, thoughtfulness, preparation, faithfulness, prayerfulness, enthusiasm, mentoring, seriousness, cheerfulness, kindness, gentleness, self-control—the Scriptures are filled with the character traits God wants to be found in His people.

9. "I will praise You, O Lord my God, with all my heart, and I will glorify Your name forevermore" (Ps. 86:12, NKJV). Wholeheartedly and continuously.

✦ Acknowledgments ✦

© Clairmont, Patsy; Johnson, Barbara; Meberg, Marilyn; and Swindoll, Luci, *Joy Breaks*, (Grand Rapids: Zondervan Publishing House, 1997)

© Clairmont, Patsy; Johnson, Barbara; Meberg, Marilyn; and Swindoll, Luci, *The Joyful Journey*, (Grand Rapids: Zondervan Publishing House, 1998)

© Clairmont, Patsy, *The Best Devotions of Patsy Clairmont*, (Grand Rapids: Zondervan Publishing House, 2001)

© Johnson, Barbara, *The Best Devotions of Barbara Johnson*, (Grand Rapids: Zondervan Publishing House, 2001)

© Meberg, Marilyn, *The Best Devotions of Marilyn Meberg*, (Grand Rapids: Zondervan Publishing House, 2001)

© Swindoll, Luci, *The Best Devotions of Luci Swindoll*, (Grand Rapids: Zondervan Publishing House, 2001)

© Walsh, Sheila, *The Best Devotions of Sheila Walsh*, (Grand Rapids: Zondervan Publishing House, 2001)

© Wells, Thelma, *The Best Devotions of Thelma Wells*, (Grand Rapids: Zondervan Publishing House, 2001)

© Women of Faith, Inc., *We Brake for Joy*, (Grand Rapids: Zondervan Publishing House, 1997)

ADDITIONAL
RESOURCES

✦ WHAT SHALL WE STUDY NEXT? ✦

**Women of Faith has three other study guides out right now
that will draw you closer to God.**

Discovering God's Will for Your Life

There are times when oh, what we wouldn't give for a little direction. Desperately we long for God's guidance. How many times have I heard people say, "I really want to do what God wants me to do, but what is it? What is His will anyway?"

Luci Swindoll

There are so many big decisions in life! Should I get married? Should we start a family? Should I stay home with my children? Should I go back to school? Should we look for a new church? Should we move? Should the kids go to a private school? Should I look for a new job? In the major choices we face throughout our lifetimes, we want so badly to do the right thing. We want to follow God's plan for our lives. We want to do God's will.

Then there are all the little decisions in life! Do I have time to join a Bible study? Should we buy a puppy? Will the car make it another year? Can we afford to give extra money for missions? Should I introduce myself to the new neighbors? Will I get tired of this wallpaper in three months? What should I make for dinner? In the little decisions of our everyday lives, does God have a plan for us too?

Well, the Bible's lessons for us are not quite so specific. We cannot turn the pages of Scripture and discover that according to 3 Hesitations 21:4 that Bernice should be a veterinarian when she grows up. However, there *are* verses that actually say "This is the will of God."

Living Above Worry and Stress

Consider the lilies, how they grow: they neither toil nor spin; and yet I say to you, even Solomon in all his glory was not arrayed like one of these. If then God so clothes the grass, which today is in the field and tomorrow is thrown into the oven, how much more will He clothe you, O you of little faith?

Luke 12:27-28, NKJV

The words echo back to us from years gone by. We first learned it in a Vacation Bible School one summer or from a dear Sunday school teacher—the voice of Jesus calling us to consider the lilies. The lesson was a simple one: don't worry. If God would give the flowers such pretty petals, dressing them more grandly than wealthy King Solomon could manage, He will provide for our needs too.

Unfortunately, the call to consider the lilies is left on a dusty shelf somewhere. It's probably right next to the old plea to stop and smell the roses. We're too busy for stopping. We're too rushed for consideration. Our "to do" lists are long. Our day timers are booked. Our time is money. We can't keep up.

We are busy people. We have responsibilities at work. We have responsibilities at home. We have responsibilities at church. We have responsibilities at school. We have responsibilities within our communities. We care for the needs of our parents, our husbands, our children, our siblings, our employers, our closest friends. Most days, it is more than we can handle. Our hearts are overwhelmed. We are stressed out. We are worried. We dread tomorrow.

In the midst of all this everyday turmoil, our hearts long for a place of peace. We know God has promised us rest. We know He says we don't have to worry about tomorrow. He promised to calm our fears. Yet we barely have time to whisper a prayer, let alone study our Bibles. If you have been struggling, come. Let's take a little time to explore the Scriptures, and find some practical guidelines for laying aside our fears, our worry, and even our stress. You really can discover a place of peace.

Adventurous Prayer: Talking with God

Prayer is reaching out to touch Someone — namely, your Creator. In the process He touches you.

Barbara Johnson

What's the big deal about prayer? We know we should all do it more often, take it more seriously, and give it more time — but we don't. Does that mean that prayer is optional? After all, some of the other spiritual disciplines seem pretty outdated, like fasting and solitude. Who has time for that? That kind of stuff is for monks, nuns, and pastors. We've gotten along okay without it.

So, does prayer fit into the *non*-essentials of the Christian walk? Prayer must be that "in case of emergency" last-resort kind of spiritual tool. Right?

Shame on you!

Prayer isn't some kind of requirement for believers. It is a privilege! You have the ear of the Divine. Prayer is our path to the adventure of building a relationship with our Savior.

God knows what's going on in your life. The Creator of all that is stoops to hear the lisping of toddlers. The Sustainer of every living thing hears the groans and sighs of the aging. He is aware of every thought, every choice, every move you make — but He is waiting for you to turn to Him and tell Him about it.

God listens to you. He will answer you.

The Complete Women of Faith™ Study Guide Series Available Now

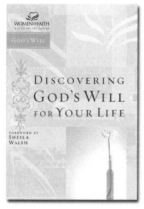

Discovering God's
Will for Your Life
0-7852-4983-4

Living Above
Worry and Stress
0-7852-4986-9

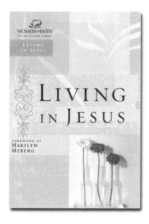

Living in Jesus
0-7852-4985-0

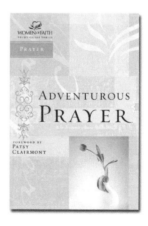

Adventurous Prayer
0-7852-4984-2

WOMEN OF FAITH®

WHO DO YOU HAVE IN MIND?

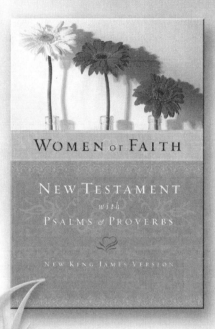

*I*ntroducing the *Women of Faith™ New Testament with Psalms & Proverbs.* Interspersed throughout the text are 24 devotionals written especially for new believers, by the well-loved Women of Faith™ conference speakers. This would truly be a wonderful gift of encouragement and hope for any new believer. So, who do you have in mind?

NKJV NEW KING JAMES VERSION®

Available at fine bookstores everywhere.

NELSON BIBLES

OTHER PRODUCTS
BY WOMEN OF FAITH™

The Great Adventure Devotional	0-8499-1775-1
Boundless Love Conference in a Box	0-8499-8383-5
Boundless Love Interactive Guide	0-8499-4379-5
Sensational Life Conference in a Box	0-8499-8384-3
Sensational Life Interactive Guide	0-8499-4423-6
The Decision of a Lifetime	0-8499-4420-1
WOF NoteTaker's Journal	1-4041-0054-7
WOF New Testament with Psalms and Proverbs	0-7180-0355-1
WOF Devotional Bible (coming Sept 2003)	0-7180-0377-2 (PB)
	0-7180-0378-0 (HC)
	0-7180-0379-9 (Leather)

Available at fine bookstores everywhere.